THE MIDDLEMAN WITH POWER:

Exploitation in the Media and Creative Arts Industries

PHUMZILE ZONKE

krest
PUBLISHERS

KREST PUBLISHERS

Copyright © Phumzile Zonke 2024
First edition

Cover Design by Monique Hayes

ISBN: 978-0-7961-5940-3 (paperback)
ISBN: 978-0-7961-5941-0 (eBook)

First published by KREST Publishers 2024

www.krestpublishers.co.za
Durban, South Africa

CONTENTS

1. The Introduction   1

2. The Creatives   17

3. The Suppliers   46

4. The Middleman   77

5. The Imbalance   148

6. *#So whART?*   154

This book is dedicated to all creative artists and broadcast media professionals who continue to grind and tell their stories in the face of empty pockets and exploitative enterprises.

1

THE INTRODUCTION

The idea of media and creative arts enterprises being intermediaries designed for the sole purpose of exploiting the very talent they employ, and maximising profit at their expense, is a historic tale comprised of anecdotal assertions that lack support from scientific evidence or empirical research. This is a sensitive topic that gets media and creative arts professionals hot under the collar, with a plethora of inconclusive questions being asked based on a tug of war between those who own the means of artistic production and distribution and those that produce the artistic ideation of media and creative arts content.

Contrary to overwhelming evidence that undoubtedly proves the commercial value and social importance of media, culture, and creative arts industries in the South African economy, to this day, there exists a relentless curse of poverty and exploitation, wherein many creative arts and media professionals suffer (alleged) unprecedented atrocities at the hands of those who own the means of creative and artistic production and distribution. Again, this is the paradoxical 'push and pull' between those that produce works of art and those that profit from them—a philosophical debate that appears to have been lost on the capitalist beings that own the production and/or distribution means, while creative artists have long accepted their defeat and succumbed to the reality of being second-class citizens that continue to plough their trade for nothing else but the sheer love of it … a phenomenon that manifests as a result of what I label 'the power of the middleman'.

In practical terms, a 'middleman' is a distinct type of fraudster known exactly as what the moniker suggests—the man in the middle. This is a person or entity that acts as an intermediary or broker during transactions between two or more parties, and who makes money by charging fees and commissions to customers in return for services rendered, such as matching buyers with sellers or moving goods and services from sellers to buyers at a pre-determined price.

The 'middleman' is utilised by both enterprises and individuals alike within the types of economic activities that enhance commercial endeavours which, in turn, accumulate power and resources through mediation of exchange between interested players, making it a concept that is often noted as a useful lens through which to amplify economic efficiency. However, although the 'middleman' concept plays an integral part in the economy (for reasons related to the ease of doing business, efficiency, speed, and convenience), the 'middleman' also remains an intermediary that is often accused of being the exploiter of both consumers and producers of goods and services alike, while on its own producing nothing of commercial value in the value chain.

It is a capitalist character in orientation that makes its profit at the alleged expense of social welfare and moral values—a corrupt character some label as the 'boogeyman' of all industries, with allegations of exploitation at all levels of the business value chain regardless of the sector being looked at. Katherine Judge, who is a professor of law at Columbia Law School in New York, argues that we are living in an era of the 'middleman' economy, where the 'middleman' plays a crucial and structural role in shaping our economies. Furthermore, this is a sentiment most people deem valid, even by the standards of developing economies like South Africa's, and despite the contrasting views that remain critical of the motives of the 'middleman', especially when levels of inequality are at an all-time high.

This remains an environment where the gap between the 'haves' and the 'have-nots' continues to widen due to the monopolistic and oligopolistic structures of our economy driven by the greed, power, and ruthlessness of the 'middleman' in order to dominate the local industries uncontested. The undeniable power of the 'middleman' has grown to unprecedented heights of success and to a multinational corporation status that drives major economic activities, with typical examples being banks, food chain retailers, fuel station retailers, broadcasting networks, major record labels, bookstore retailers, and so on and so forth.

International conglomerates have invested heavily in technology and infrastructure to distribute goods and services at a large scale and at price levels determined by them, which is a logical practice designed to ease the process of doing business. That is, until one takes a closer look at the system and realises how concentrated it really is. But be that as it may, this book focuses mostly on broadcasting—the creative arts industry where most of this 'middleman' pandemic prevails unabated, and where the 'middleman' is a veiled concept that is mostly downplayed and normalised by all creative stakeholders involved, including artists themselves who are the prime victims of this ecosystem. In the entertainment industry, the 'middleman' would constitute enterprises such as record labels, broadcast networks, and online streaming platforms, to name just a few.

Large record labels, such as Universal Music Group, Sony Music Entertainment, and Warner Music Group, who are often labelled as the 'majors', reign supreme as major controllers of the entertainment market, with uncontested power over artists and music business affairs. These are the types of institutions that are generally accused of breeding the culture of 'struggling artists' who spend most of their professional life scrambling for any jobs they can find just to put food on the table, whereas the owners of production and distribution means are swimming in wealth and riches off the backs of the poor artists' creative labour. However, many would also argue this as nothing but a conspiracy theory stemming from those on the outside of economic activity in the creative arts industry.

The broadcasting industry said to be toxic and plagued with a myriad of socioeconomic challenges resembling uncertainty, inconsistency, and unreliability, and it is an industry filled with a plethora of artists pretending to be millionaires drowning in luxury, fame, and fortune (if their social media presence is anything to go by). The unfortunate reality is that the 'starving artist' concept has long been embedded in our society, even before the penniless Vincent Van Gogh earned his place in history as a tragic artistic genius who never saw the fortunes his long-suffering creative pursuits came to be worth. A broad acceptance of this enduring stereotype contributes to how much society considers the lives of struggling artists who experience financial hardships and lack the necessary business skills to sustain a creative profession.

The creative arts struggle is a tale as old as time, wherein plying one's trade in the arts can be both rewarding and unsympathetic, invoking images of starving artists and a ruthless 'jungle'—a term coined to vividly depict the exploitative industry that preys on the martyrdom of artists whose preoccupation with producing art appears to eclipse sound business judgment. The starving artist paradigm, I argue, finds its roots in all forms of the arts, which have yielded some of our most inspiring cultural contributions. Yet, many artists who give us these treasures often die in disgrace, only recognised after their deaths as cultural icons whose achievements failed to yield financial successes during their lifetimes. They even sometimes die as a result of depression and suicide following an invariable conclusion that there is no way out, as everyone including family, friends, fans, and the media has turned their backs on them … some even putting a final nail in the coffin by ensuring that these people continue to profit financially through royalties and repeat fee proceeds that were never really enjoyed by the deceased.

For most of our socioeconomic lives, art has always been a manifestation of our deepest dreams, desires, and anxieties. Artists work for their passions but unfortunately do so in a world where money dictates the narrative and relegates passion to something that is never enough to sustain a proper livelihood, therein demonstrating total disregard for the fact that artists are as much a part of society as individuals working in any other industry are. The real cause of exploitation couldn't be more underrated and unacknowledged due to artists and society conveniently refusing to consider it important enough to discuss … that is, until an artist tragically dies from depression attributed to the persistent struggle to survive and make a living as a professional.

This is a sad state of affairs that receives the spotlight only when a death occurs and, all of a sudden, the public appears willing to discuss the plight of starving artists and the abuse that persists uncontested while the 'middleman' smiles all the way to the bank. Here, too, our government officials jump on the bandwagon, dishing out empty promises while artists continue to normalise the abnormality of the situation, giving breath to the problem by being silent and venting only in dark corridors, while every refuted agreement, every withheld payment, and every rejected credit is detrimental to the creative arts industry as a whole.

Irrespective of what shape or form it takes, exploitation is a brutal labour precarity performed by those in power—and those who own the production and distribution means—to subtly treat artists unjustly. For instance, creative ideas of the artists are sometimes stolen and commercialised without their consent or permission, verbal and written agreements are dishonoured and artists manipulated into doing more than the stipulated amount of work, and some are compelled to even perform sexual favours in exchange for jobs or little moments of fame that never translate to monetary rewards.

One of the striking anomalies of the media and the creative arts industry is this two-faced character of the creative arts economy. On the one hand, the splendour of magnificent fame and fortune is depicted, wherein artists earn lucrative endorsement deals and rake in high streams of income while enjoying the status that comes with being rich, famous, and surrounded by glitz and glamour. On the other hand, however, and contrary to popular belief, many of these artists live below the poverty line and earn very little, if anything at all—a phenomenon that results in some creative artists taking on additional jobs as waiters/waitresses, cleaners, call centre agents, joining pyramid schemes, and, more recently, trying out the cunning forex trading scams.

The veiled economic system of the media and creative arts industry amplifies an undeniable false reality of splendour, fame, and fortune, which actually ends up breeding artists' poverty and strips them of their dignity and freedom to make a sustainable living. Meanwhile, others resort to moving in with their relatives (a decision that comes with its own sense of shame and stigma), and those in stable, intimate relationships resort to accepting support from their partners. In extreme instances, some even end up staying in abusive relationships due to their inability to take care of themselves and their loved ones. Artists have nowhere else to go while their chosen career path continues showing poor signs of enough growth to help them make a living and contribute meaningfully to the economy.

I classify this kind of indignity as the systematic shackles of the creative arts economy that are in place primarily as a result of the so-called 'middleman' while also being driven by the very same artists' complicity in these industry shenanigans that are parasitic to their well-being, under the 'middleman's' invisible hand of profit maximisation and bottom-line agenda. Herein lies a serious conundrum of the creative arts industry. Profit motives are merely veiled in public, and commercial and economic aspects remain denied and condemned by the so-called proponents of 'art for a good cause', thereby driving the gift sphere value system agenda that encourages selflessness camouflaged as devotion to art and condemns the pursuit of monetary gains. This is a concerning form of hypocrisy that masquerades as public good while hiding behind the gift sphere value system analogy that appears more valued and is expressed more openly in the arts sector.

However, similar to other, more 'traditional' industries, transactions are still guided by the average market values of commercialisation. Hence, it boggles the mind as to why the topic of money remains a 'taboo' in the creative arts industry, being veiled and deemed inappropriate. A discourse, I assert, that plays itself beautifully into the hands of the 'middleman' to exploit the gap and create an opportunity for commercial gain. It makes no sense that artists who exhibit anti-market values and position themselves as proponents of vocation and 'calling euphoria' are applauded for authenticity and for doing the right thing for the public good, while at the same time they are crying themselves to sleep due to starvation and the inability to make a living. This despicable level of immorality deserves condemnation of the highest order, especially in the backdrop of statistics which reveal that, according to the South African Cultural Observatory, cultural and creative arts industries' gross value added (GVA) was at about R161 billion in 2020, contributing R90 billion to the gross domestic product (GDP) and representing around three percent of total economic production in South Africa that year, putting it almost on par with the agricultural sector.

If anything, this encouragement of an anti-market/anti-commercialisation mindset appears to be a self-imposed form of brainwashing that gives a false sense of the enhancement of artists' market value and brand equity as a result of pushing the 'love of arts' narrative, while the artist will end up dying poor in the name of the arts, again opening the very same floodgate for the 'middleman' to exploit them for organisational financial prosperity. This conundrum also makes me wonder, *Why is the creative arts market so hell-bent on wanting artists to pretend they are being done a favour when they are getting paid what is rightfully owed to them?* Deliberately omitting the conversation about money and avoiding putting a price on the artists' value and quality of their work in a standardised and regulated manner is denying the arts economy the right to grow, professionalise, and be competitive.

Everyone knows that there is no such thing as a market rate for creative artists in South Africa. The price tag of a creative artist and their services rendered in South Africa is a highly subjective idea that is dependent on who is in front of you, which creates a very dysfunctional business environment that operates differently to other sectors. Hence, the ultimate plea this book seeks to make is the creation of a normal market where the remuneration of artists is not dependent on who they know and/or who they are, but rather on the performance, skills, and experience they bring to the table. A space where artists are not demonised and labelled as 'divas' or 'big headed' for claiming to know their value and demanding what they believe is their worth. An industry where economic principles of supply and demand dictated by the market determines pricing in order to achieve fairness. An environment where artists' credentials determine whether they get a job or whether they become the highest-paid artist on set.

As much as there are artists out there that we know earn relatively well despite the 'starving artist' trope dominating popular culture, evidence actually indicates that the average income among artists is comparatively lower than other professions in South Africa—a phenomenon that suggests taking up art as a profession in this country is financial suicide, where an artist walks in knowing that they are about to endure what some scholars call the 'income penalty'. The arts is a precarious industry that presents a high probability of dreams deferred and unfulfilled aspirations of being rich and famous. Hans Abbing—a social scientist, published author, and expert in the economy of the arts—said in his 2002 article "Why are Artists Poor?" that "It's not just proven skills that determine whether someone becomes an artist; someone's inadequacies can also be just as important." An argument suggesting that artists may choose to become artists not because of their creative/artistic superiority and expertise, but because they believe they are unfit to do anything else professionally.

Abbing also argued that, "The low income that characterizes many creative art careers across the globe is partly displayed by artists' beliefs that they themselves lack the ordinary skills necessary for non-creative and artistic professions," which further suggests that the non-professionalisation of the creative arts industry is a self-orchestrated disaster that is manifested by the same so-called creative artists who choose their profession due to their perceived inability to do anything else ... an assertion I believe very few creative artists would take kindly to.

However, with all that is said and done about how dysfunctional the creative arts industry is—and how brutal it has been and continues to be towards artists in the hands of what I call the 'middleman'—the reality of it all is that the creative companies who often contract the services of artists are actually struggling enterprises themselves and are themselves being exploited by the *new* 'middleman' that has emerged as a result of new digital technologies enabled by the growth of the internet and universal access. Music, film, and television industries are the prime examples of this power shift, where record labels specifically have now found themselves having to figure out new strategies to deal with the idea of large technological, multinational platforms that allow musicians to trade directly with those who consume the music, including Spotify, Apple Music, Amazon, Deezer, etc. Similarly, the growth of over-the-top (OTT) video streaming platforms, such as Netflix, Amazon Prime Video, and Disney+, is having the same effect on linear and network satellite broadcast platforms, where the traditional 'middleman' (in the form of 'majors' and public broadcasting enterprises) is cut out and replaced with a new form of 'middleman' that appears to be offering filmmakers, producers, screenwriters, etc., better revenue proceeds and autonomy in the marketing and ownership of their product.

In the audiovisual broadcast industry, creative performers, such as actors and presenters, cry about the same things musicians complain about, most of them levelling their accusations at the film and television production houses for being hell bent on paying creative artists and technical crews peanuts while also treating them as easily disposable cogs in a machine that can be replaced in the blink of an eye if they don't perform their required function. One would think this a form of exploitation in which (if you follow the 'middleman' logic) film and television production houses are the 'middlemen' looting and abusing creatives and playing a demigod between creatives and the broadcast networks. However, we then come to the realisation that production houses are themselves the major victims of a rigged broadcast ecosystem that abuses them, rips them off, and leaves them with no bargaining power, low costs per *mille* (CPMs), unrealistic deadlines, and alleged bribing requirements they are subjected to at the hands of commissioning editors and program managers in order to get contracts. A veiled 'take it or leave it' mafia-style operation, and an impossibly toxic supplier-client relationship, is thereby created in the industry that trickles down to all spheres of the value chain, eventually affecting technical crew and creative talent the most.

The production house-broadcast network relationship imbalance is probably one of the most concealed and unspoken complexities in the industry, with many perhaps not even knowing it exists and others choosing not to enter that discussion at all due to the fear of victimisation and isolation. The same exploitation creative artists complain about against production houses and record labels is experienced by these film and television production houses/producers. As suppliers of content, they actually suffer the same problems (if not worse ones) based on the number of different stakeholders they are accountable to and who are expecting the show to go on regardless of their level of dissatisfaction, and because they themselves are easily disposable hand-to-mouth companies the broadcaster can replace at a snap of a finger. A phenomenon that also presents broadcast networks as the real 'middleman' with enormous financial muscle and power to dictate and control the economic activities of the audio-visual industry, such as who does or doesn't get the job and at what price the job is offered and valued.

The audio-visual industry is a highly concentrated one with an oligopolistic system infested with so much corruption and cronyism, and where 'wheeling and dealing' is the order of the day. It is an industry that has become so sophisticated in normalising dysfunction to a point where everyone involved accepts it as a valid business norm that no one could ever disprove nor do anything about, but rather just feel in every corner of the industry. A culture like this, I suppose, takes many years of experience to perfect and demands high levels of trust among those that are in the 'inner circle' and are bestowed with the responsibility of keeping it tightly protected (or gatekept) for the benefit of a select few charlatans. However, for argument's sake, let's assume this is nothing but a conspiracy theory and that I am, hypothetically, just a disgruntled producer who hasn't benefitted from this system after thousands of unsuccessful pitches to broadcast networks across the country.

How would you then explain the commissioning of the same *telenovela* for more than ten seasons on prime time, with the accumulative budget value being upwards of R1 billion, while the audience ratings are displaying a negative trajectory into depressing territories in terms of viewership? How can that kind of strategic decision make any business sense for a broadcaster who is likely also receiving thousands of unsolicited proposals and conceptual pitch decks to revamp their schedules and editorial output? The only possible conclusion is that there is perhaps an invisible hand at play between certain content suppliers and broadcasters—the 'middleman'.

Considering the fact that there are more than 3 000 production houses in the Gauteng province alone, imagine all 3 000 pitching and submitting unsolicited proposals to the tune of thousands every day to all the country's broadcast networks, only for these networks to continue working with the same handful of under-performing suppliers. This is sadly a common business practice these days in the video and entertainment industry, defended under the guise of sticking with experienced suppliers who are tried and tested in order to mitigate the liability of newness. I supposed this practice makes sense when, as a business, you are genuinely trying to protect your investment and avoid unnecessary risk, but this becomes suspect when some content suppliers (i.e., production houses) with no experience and, in extreme cases, who have not even produced a single thirty-second clip in their creative lives, are given an opportunity to produce intricate technical and specialist prime-time drama series that we all know require expert knowledge and years of experience with heavy investment.

That throws the entire argument out the window and positions the 'middleman' as nothing but a crony who is in collusion with a select few content suppliers for personal gains completely unrelated to the superior, innovative creative concepts at hand and the industry growth of an enterprise or network's profitability. It presents the unintended consequences of compromised quality and erodes audiences over time, as the drivers of this practice are often not operating in the interest of the business as a whole. Every producer talks about this corrupt business practice in the corridors and how it has turned most of them into hand-to-mouth beggars that spend most of their lives queuing at the Department of Arts and Culture just to get pilot funding they can use as a bargaining chip to prove their worth and attract additional funds to produce a real piece of work. The system is totally broken, and it yields a domino effect where the scarcity of funds and the concentration of those who are lucky enough to get the commissioning contracts pass down the scarcity syndrome to every sphere of the business, which, in turn, results in the creative artists employed by production houses suffering the financial penalty and exploitative labor conditions that stem from the aforementioned calamity.

To paint the picture for those who might not get the scale of this challenge the creative arts enterprises face: Where, on average, a market-related, thirty-second long television spot or advert would cost a commercial brand R10 million to deliver in a space of four weeks, a producer of long-form content is subjected to deals where, on average, R70 million rand is a 'take it or leave it' deal for them to deliver a *telenovela* comprising 260 episodes, with each episode constituting twenty-four minutes. How broadcasters expect production houses to create cash flow and still deliver without exploiting and/ or cutting down on any aspects of the production is astonishing. This scenario perfectly depicts the abusive nature of the media creative arts industry in the hands of the 'middlemen' (broadcasters) and how it doesn't care about the way production houses make things happen, as long as they deliver the content at the prescribed levels of quality and by the predetermined deadlines (or what we call 'TX dates' in television). Another common business practice across the creative arts industry is that, after all is said and done and the completed production is delivered to the broadcasters, the production company has nothing to show for it except for appearing in the credits. They possess no intellectual property rights nor revenue share options; instead, they go back to the drawing board— queuing for the next brief, pitching new concepts, and praying for the audience ratings performance to be favorable so that they can be in line for recommission (if they are in the commissioning editors' or program managers' good books, that is).

This picture appears unfair, abusive, and squarely places all the power and influence in the hands of the 'middleman' where broadcasting is concerned. Therefore, it is a no-brainer why the culture, media, and creative arts industry appears stagnant and is squeezing most of the talented creatives out, with some shifting their careers to academia and others joining political parties to try their luck with government tenders. This is notwithstanding the latest trend where creative artists are now starting non-governmental organisations (NGOs) that pretend to be helping and developing disadvantaged communities or training others that want to enter the industry—a very suspicious move that has recently been reported as yet another scam wherein the government officials that facilitate such funds are in collusion with some so-called 'celebrities' to embezzle these resources for their own self-enrichment, and it is a phenomenon that appears prevalent in all spheres of the creative arts industry, including both musical artists as well as film and TV artists. If these methods don't work, some artists end up resorting to shifting their focus towards foreign funding options and international festivals for marketing and fundraising opportunities, as they have largely lost hope and given up on the local market.

2

THE CREATIVES

Something most of us have forgotten is that a world without creatives is a world without courage, passion, and realised dreams, and a world filled with nothing but pure emptiness and no imagination to take any country's creative economy forward. Take, for example, the music industry. Since the beginning of time, people have enjoyed music through the physical attendance of live performances—a moment in time where artists would perform to small audiences that were able to travel as far as their feet could carry them, and a mode of creative delivery that carried on up until the entrance of technological discontinuity into the market several years ago, which was a transformation that played a crucial role in enabling the performing artists to expand their work to larger audiences in a new, unprecedented way. Radio technology actually pioneered this evolution and allowed musicians to reach anyone that could access the airwaves, while the seminal gramophone system allowed music to be replayed infinitely without the physical presence of the musician or artist; all this in the quest for incremental improvements to advance the loyalty to and reach of music, and with the objective of recreating the experience of a live performance while conveying it to the widest and the furthest audience possible.

This phenomenon, however, has always come at a significant cost, particularly for artists who wanted to access the largest audiences the technological discontinuities could offer. It is a market development which has engineered a scenario wherein musical artists enter into agreements with radio stations and record labels who, in turn, have made investments towards owning and controlling these technologies. A trajectory that resulted in an industry boom where most of the rich and successful musicians were born, sparking a sense of prosperity where their inherent talents found expression and were enhanced by the technological developments of the time which allowed them to bring their best selves (their 'A' game) in front of the largest audiences that would never have been reachable before.

However, as exciting as this evolution has been, specifically for the music industry, the tradeoff for this technological transformation, and the privilege of using the technology, is that creative artists had to enter into agreements where they were made to share a significant portion of their earnings with the record labels—a development that most artists didn't appreciate but had no choice but to comply with, as most of them didn't have the necessary resources to forward their careers on their own. Despite this, as time went by, many of these same artists grew to be larger-than-life personalities and took offense at the manner in which record labels were controlling and treating them. They took matters into their own hands, deciding to grab the bull by the horns by speaking their truth to power and protesting publicly against the industry in an attempt to wrestle back their power and control from the bureaucrats (colloquially known as the 'suits'). However, the advent of a new technological discontinuity forced them, yet again, into another seismic shift of the music industry.

This, of course, refers to the digital transformation shift of the music industry, a place in time muddied by nothing but mediocrity in its inception, and an operation that was hamstrung by compression technologies and limited bandwidth in a period where early digital music was practically unusable. Yet, despite such shortcomings and sometimes patent illegalities, some digital enterprises selling the product were runaway successes, with users of such platforms prepared to trade off the poor sound quality that came with CDs, for example, just to gain access to the audiences these platforms offered. While a game changing moment, this was also a problematic era of the music industry wherein music was made available free of charge, which deprived not only record labels of their revenue but musical artists as well. This was a trajectory that predictably resulted in some tightening of the laws and bolstering of enforcement to reduce piracy, a phenomenon that essentially brought forth the notion of digital music distribution into the mainstream and renewed focus on improving reliability and better compression technology that would set digital music apart from the primitive era of vinyl records.

This represents an industry development that has finally moved music distribution out of the control of the traditional music industry and straight to the hands of the large technology enterprises, such as Google, Amazon, Apple, and recently Spotify, to name just a few. These are the types of multinational enterprises that continue to leverage their digital platforms by offering enormous collections of music, initially through digital downloads and eventually via subscription business models. This is the world we now live in, a moment in time where we no longer own music but stream it via on-demand services and platforms that allow us to access it wherever we are and whenever we feel the need, finally providing artists with access to the largest possible audiences on the planet.

While appearing exciting at face value, this evolution leaves us with inconclusive questions that remain unanswered: "Why is it that artists' margins remain at the lowest levels they have ever been despite the evolutional improvements of the technology and the limitless access to global markets?" Here, we again have a tug of war that points directly to the record label as a 'middleman' that still owns an immense amount of music catalogues in exchange for the rights to stream musical content—a system that continues to enable record labels to retain a significant share of the music revenue (which all comes directly from the artists' own revenue and creative prowess), and a mind-staggering dichotomy where, in 2024, one wonders why these prevailing intermediaries still exist between the artists and their audience.

It becomes an especially pertinent question now that technology has democratised music production to a point where even the poorest of the poor can produce studio-quality recordings on a personal laptop from a backroom shack in the townships, exhibit A being the establishment and disruption of the *Amapiano* genre that has blown the market wide open, not only for local consumers but for the rest of the world to enjoy as well. Proof that through social media and internet marketing, one is able to be far more impactful as an artist than if one were relying on the traditional techniques and strategies recording labels still rely on. This, again, presents an inconclusive quagmire that begs further questions on why we are still beholden to the idea of an industry that seems to be so out of touch and has lost its relevance.

Rahul Matthan, published author and speaker on matters related to emerging technologies and the law, attempts to answer these questions by arguing that, perhaps, "The answer lies in the fact that there is lack of alternatives in the music industry," which is an assertion, I argue, that stems squarely from corruption, exploitation, and manipulation of the artists' desire to obtain fame and fortune—a *modus operandi* where record labels care more about their own bottom line and less about the financial wellbeing of the creative artists. This is unfortunately a fundamental reality not unique to the music industry but common in all other sectors of the creative economy as well, including the film and television sector. However, Matthan also laments on the fact that blockchain technology based on 'pay-per-play' services is the latest and probably best bet for musicians/artists to cut out the 'middleman' and get their music directly into the hands of their audiences without the need for intermediaries (the 'boogeymen'). We are in an absolute prime time for musicians to take matters into their own hands and engage in trade deals which embrace smart contracts powered by Bitcoin or other cryptocurrencies and which allow music consumers/fans to decide how much they want to pay per stream and ensure that every bit of that revenue is automatically transferred to all the artists who played on the track in whatever proportion they'd agreed upon in the contract.

A proposition like this, I suppose, could be the final piece in an age-old puzzle to eradicate artist exploitation and financial screwing once and for all, although this is a proposition not yet accepted by the artists themselves, let alone the music industry. This is partly because, central to most problems faced by musicians in the music industry, artists themselves can be their own worst enemies and are often not interested in these discussions. They prefer to simply be left alone to focus on what they do best, which is to see to the creative parts of the business and be paid well for it, hoping that anything other than music creation can be delegated to someone else—an unfortunate behavior that opens them up to abuse, exploitation, and manipulation, for the 'middleman' to defraud the revenue that should have been accrued to them.

In the era of the digital economy, every scholar will tell you (including even ten-year-old kids) that the internet has blown most creative industries wide open and created lucrative business opportunities that never existed before. The music industry is no different. It has now become common knowledge that the role of the 'middleman' (played by the record labels) to produce, distribute, and promote albums is dead and has been emphatically compromised by the internet, much to the benefit of artists and music consumers. Social media platforms have parachuted many relatively unknown bands and musical groups into instant celebrity status through online publicity and viral content strategies—like international stars Justin Bieber and Shawn Mendes who got their big breaks on YouTube, and even local *Amapiano* artist Kamo Mphela who made a name for herself on social media during the COVID-19 pandemic—boosting the sales of their independently produced music and downloads and aggressively eliminating the need for a major record label to promote their work, in turn allowing them to sell fewer copies of their music and still make far more money than they could have done through a label. The internet has not only pulled the rug under the feet of the 'boogeyman' in the name of record labels, but it has also provided low-cost online distribution—an inspiring evolution where digital technology also reduces the cost of production, with *Amapiano* again being a testament to this. Online distribution channels/platforms are proof beyond reasonable doubt of the fatality of the traditional 'boogeyman' of the music industry known as record labels, and they have created room for a new form of bigger and better 'middleman', which inadvertently places artists that still prefer to do business with record labels in a better and more positive position to negotiate better deals.

For the longest time, creative artists have been crying and complaining about how corrupted and rigged the system has been, with some of us accusing them of being spoilt brats who misuse their money when they are at the peak of their careers, only to cry foul when they are down and out and have lost their relevance. However, we know now that creatives have never been crazy; it's the so-called critics of the arts and proponents of capital that never cared to dig deeper and look at the inherent issues through the artists' eyes. We are at a moment in time where artists are now spoilt for choice and can take full charge of their music careers if they so choose. The reduction of production and distribution costs through the internet and digital technology has thus transformed the music industry from one with fixed, unaffordable costs of promotion, distribution, and medium marginal production into one with low, flexible costs in promotion and very low marginal costs of production and distribution.

There are still alternative schools of thought in relation to the 'middleman' concept who argue that going directly to the source is not just a naïve call to cut out the 'middleman', but it is a response to the demand for cheaper goods and services and for greater convenience of both consumers and suppliers. I agree that this assertion is not entirely incorrect, although I am skeptical of the underlying motives therein, judging by how most of these 'middlemen' have behaved over the years, and it would be naïve to think that the artists would let things go without a fight.

However, despite the opportunities to go direct and cut out the 'middleman', the 'boogeyman' is here to stay and believes it plays a critical role in facilitating the flow of goods and services from those who have them to those who want them. Hence, the proponents of the 'middleman' business model, alongside its beneficiaries, argue that the goal should never be to eliminate the 'middleman' system in the creative arts industries completely, but rather understand the value it brings and the danger it poses so that we can achieve a healthier balance. My question is, "What balance?" What balance are we referring to when most artists continue to die as paupers without even a cent to bury themselves, while the 'middleman' is swimming in wealth and fortune and blaming artists for not managing their finances adequately? Where were these values and the *healthy balance* when artists were alive and crying for help?

The truth of the matter is that the 'middleman' has become way too large, powerful, and complex for its own good. This has even become evident in the banking sector, where most of us suffer ridiculous banking charges from this 'boogeyman' who is enabled by the state regulatory remits. The same can be said for fuel companies, food retailers, broadcast networks, publishing houses, and many more. All of them are accused of perpetuating inequalities and giving poverty a face, and we have every reason to make sure that the 'middleman' economy is a thing of the past regardless of the sector of operation.

At any chance creative artists get, their sole objective should be to abandon the 'middleman' concept, as it has proven itself, for centuries, as being incapable of taking accountability and as caring for no one but its own bottom line, with artists being nothing but collateral damage of a looting spree between them and the selected corrupt suppliers. Thanks to digital technology and new distribution channels, more creatives and consumers now have a direct relationship and can render the 'middleman' redundant and openly undermine its dominance.

Creatives remain at the centre of this network of people working in collaborations directly or indirectly to generate profits. Like any other business with a solid online presence and relying on digital technologies for its advancements, it is also expected in the creative arts business that it will become more complex for additional stakeholders to enter the ecosystem. These innovative developments, however, are welcomed in the creative arts industry and come with great opportunities and vulnerabilities alike, with areas of development that still warrant discussions on proverbial exploitation of the creatives, even during the era of digital and technological advancements that seek to take power back from the 'boogeyman' into the hands of the creatives themselves.

Creative industries need to stop selling the 'glitz and glamour' façade to creative artists when the reality is that this is an industry plagued with famously opaque, litigious, and corrupt practices of the 'middleman'. Issa Rae, well-known American actress, writer, and producer, further asserts that creative industries are ones that appear unstructured, unprofessional, unregulated, and as a "free-for-all" to loot and exploit for selfish gains and myopic capitalist ends that leave creatives starving, miserable, and depressed.

However, some could also argue that perhaps ignorance of the creatives themselves in relation to copyright laws and publishing rights is one of the reasons they struggle to make it in the industry and subsequently suffer in the hands of the 'boogeyman'. It's high time that someone tells the creatives that artistic talent alone is no longer enough to guarantee longevity and sustainability in this industry. It is actually the combination of creative and entrepreneurial skills that is the magic wand which will empower artists with incredible expertise, allowing them to pivot new strategies that can keep them in the game and remain relevant and competitive without the purported expertise and economies of scale offered by the 'middleman'.

As unregulated and unstructured as this industry might appear to be, there is still a system among the madness. As witnessed in previous years, this remains an industry that has a way of rejecting and isolating 'fly-by-night' chance-takers that are only seeking celebrity status and have no sense of artistic self-expression and innate skills to make it to the top. Content consumers are brutal clients who will easily and quickly detect and demonstrate to you how talentless you are and why you don't belong in the game, but because artists are often the most passionate workers, and given the 'middleman' economy of the arts, creatives are the ones likely to be taken advantage of. Passion is always the easiest and the softest area used by the 'boogeyman' to justify exploitation.

Passion for one's work should ordinarily lead to greater satisfaction and better rewards. Instead, research on personality and social psychology argues that attributions of passion serve as a tool to legitimise the poor treatment of workers, a narrative that suggests that managers and owners of the means of production tend to ask passionate workers to work extra hours without additional pay, sacrifice their family time, and sometimes take on demeaning tasks outside of their job description or scope of work. This is a treatment synonymous with what the 'middlemen' of the creative arts and media industries would do to exploit their creative human capital.

A common misconception assumes that if someone loves their job, they will prefer to work endlessly instead of performing other activities that contribute to the fulfilment of their lives. However, most creative artists have not realised that their passion could be the source of their exploitation by the 'middleman'. Whereas the 'middleman' has discovered that artists take pleasure in writing songs and performing on stage and has taken the opportunity to milk them as much as they can while publicly paddling the idea that being an artist is a privilege they should be grateful for. Creatives of all disciplines need to avoid presenting their craft as a calling or passion, as this is often used as a code-word for exploitation and abusive conditions. How often have you heard managers say, "If you are looking for money from this job, walk away; we need passionate people that are prepared to work long hours and work under pressure"? This is the insanity of desperation that creatives themselves enable in fear of not being able to ever get a job if they refuse to comply.

At the apex of this conversation is the lack of understanding of the value creatives have and the subsequent relinquishing of their power to the 'middleman' whose sole purpose is to preserve and operate in the interests of the company. According to labour expert and law professor Veena Dubal, "The increased expectation of one's passion has become a cultural justification for an economic trend to undercut workers' protection. The idea of passion underlies the 'be your own boss' rhetoric of gig companies alike who often depict the work as a side hustle for passionate people pursuing bigger dreams and therefore not really a job."

This cultural phenomenon needs to change, and creatives need to push back and unite among themselves instead of waiting for someone else to come to the rescue. News flash! No one is coming. If creatives, particularly artists, don't take ownership of their industries and begin to clean out all the cronies and criminals in the form of 'middlemen' (and the beneficiaries of these boys-only 'boogeyman' clubs), looting and exploitation will continue unabated, and these conversations will be nothing but mere talk shows. Creatives need to take ownership of their business. The creative arts economy is only partly passion and mostly business, meaning that something ought to be said about the type of training these creative artists and media practitioners get from the media arts schools that prepare them for the markets.

Institutions of higher learning are also to be blamed for the exploitative behaviour taking place in the creative arts and media industries, raising proverbial questions about the level of business and entrepreneurial education that is being imparted to media and arts students in preparation for their future so they can manage, lead, distribute, package, position, strategise, compete, and negotiate their own contracts. There should be emphasis on modules that sharpen their skills on creative leadership, brand building, marketing, diversification strategy, financial management, entertainment law or contracting, negotiating, regulations, political economy, etc.

These types of skills that can never be separated from creatives, for by virtue of being an artist or a creative, you are a business that ought to be developed, packaged, positioned, distributed, sold, and benchmarked against similar products. As an artist, you are no different from any product or service that is already on the market. The problem is that most artists just wake up in the morning and tell themselves that they are artists, with no self-diagnosis or situational analysis to survey the market they want to enter, or to project their probability of success against the existing competition in order to evaluate the capabilities and resources at their disposal to gain competitive advantage and increase their profit-making potential. We all wake up thinking we can sing, dance, write, and/or act, only to then find ourselves deep in the proverbial matrix of failure and depression.

The goal is not to create commercial specialists out of the creative practitioners, but rather to prepare creatives for the entrepreneurial orientation of their industry. Imparting the basic fundamentals of commerce could assist them in short-circuiting the 'middleman' reliance, thereby rebooting the industry dysfunctions right from the source of the problem, which I argue is the educational gap emanating from the training these creatives acquire. This is an intervention that I assert would make it very difficult for the 'middleman' to exploit them. The fight for fair remuneration of creative professionals and adequate accrual of royalties and repeat fees is not an unreasonable request.

Creative professionals need to grab the bull by the horns and start hustling for ownership of their craft. However, this can only happen when they treat themselves as entrepreneurs and as owning their businesses, instead of fronting for the endorsement of other people's enterprises. I often got excited when I saw creative artists launching alcohol brands, perfumes, clothing ranges, sneakers, etc., until I discovered that they actually owned no stake in the transaction; they were just paid to be the face of the brand and help push sales—a clear indication that there is indeed incredible value to their brand as artists, and hence why everyone is lining up to leverage off of their fame for profit maximisation. Now, imagine if the creative artists were doing this for themselves, and imagine the level of wealth that they could potentially accumulate. American artists do this all the time and do it successfully. Consider, for instance, the number of makeup and beauty companies that have been started by American female popstars, including Rihanna's 'Fenty Beauty', Selena Gomez's 'Rare Beauty', and Ariana Grande's 'R.E.M. Beauty'. Other than the high financial resources required, what else is prohibiting creative artists from doing things like this for themselves?

If a traditional organisation can acknowledge that it has a cash-flow deficit but has a particular product/service on offer that is projected to have a particular sale or revenue generation, and it has made clear the value of its assets, infrastructure, and skilled team of qualified experts to pivot, track, monitor, and evaluate the trajectory in the quest for positive returns for shareholders, why is it so difficult for artists to say, "Although I have a cash flow deficit, with my artistic piece of work never before seen on the market that has projected potential to gain traction nationwide, and with the equipment, skills, and team of qualified experts to help me pivot my brand to positive territories, can you invest in me?" This is the entrepreneurial acumen required from artists that could make them stake their ground and take control of their business. As creatives, we need to change how we think about ourselves and the role we play (or ought to be playing) in the market, alongside how we are perceived as professionals.

Ideas are the new currency, and creative artists possess a wealth of incredible ideas. It has been said that all the riches and achievements in the world begin with an idea—a resource creatives already possess in abundance. If they can be put out there on the market for public consumption without even knowing if they will be good or bad, that is a high-risk business synonymous with the entrepreneurship theory, which confirms how creatives should be looking at themselves moving forward. Accepting that, while companies possess physical properties, creative artists possess *intellectual* properties that can be classified as non-real estate wealth.

This is a cultural product that brings wealth to our country through exploitation and preservation of culture, wealth in attitude, a wealth of courage, and products that are produced for the market to heal the nation during times of despair. The era of talented creatives that never take this journey because of the fear of being broke and starving to death must come to an end. Like any other entrepreneurship endeavour, creative artists continue to laugh in the face of empty pockets and do so through the wealth of resilience, standing witness to many creatives who never say they are broke but rather investing in their future. It is disheartening to see how society and the system lacks belief in the value and the appreciation of art and fails to cultivate an industry of talented artists classified as entrepreneurs.

However, there is also a certain capitalist belief that art and business don't mix, with some arguing that creative independence and stakeholder accountability can never appear in the same sentence. News flash! Business and art have always been in a union since time immemorial; creative artists have just always been excluded from the conversation and only allowed to focus on what is coined their 'passion' or 'calling' while the 'middleman' takes care of the business and commercial side of the art as a product or service being sold.

It is imperative that creatives shake off the celebrity persona and refuse to rely solely on their chosen form of art. They need to let go of their preconceived ideas and recognise that times have changed—a single source of income these days is no longer enough. This is not to advocate for slavery and low-earning side hustles, but is rather to advocate for diversification strategies that can yield additional streams of income in pursuit of ownership of the production means, ensuring that every project attached to you and your brand is anchored on the premise that any kind of work you do is creatively fulfilling and commercially rewarding towards your financial freedom, even long after the 'songs of the year' lists and Broadway standing ovations are over and the celebrity-status novelty has worn off.

The philosophy of income diversity is the new trend for survival; hence, you will hear people talking about side hustles even in corporate settings. Similar to the concept of a side hustle, one needs to think beyond one's passion for artistic production, dance, acting, or presenting and use this window of popularity to acquire resources in the form of capital, infrastructure, networks, and all forms of production means. Being a creative artist these days is no longer what it's cracked up to be, and it's not where the money is. Hence, most brands are now shifting to influencers for numbers, as most of the time, real creative artists are never the ones that trend on social media platforms nor possess huge followings in terms of likes and comments. These are the brutal realities of our market discontinuities, where posting your sex tape could make you an overnight sensation and a celebrity for a week. Skotty Fairclough, a musician who goes by the name 'Hey Skotty', argues that if someone is a creative, and that's what they want to do, they must just do it or they'll forever wonder what could have been.

It's not always all about the money. Sometimes it's about going for it and letting the unknown take you on a life-long journey of freedom that money could never buy, he says. "It's about creating your own destiny, not having a boss, experiencing life's extremes of highs and lows, living in cars, finding money when you have none, experiencing the generosity of strangers and channelling those moments back into your art. It's the travel, the adventure, finding doorways only such a life of unknown certainty could open. Problem-solving, overcoming adversity and reflecting on how far you have come from where you began," he continues.

Lamenting that, if you merely want to create your own music but don't want to do things on someone else's terms, Skotty then says, "Don't avoid the hard tasks, or ignore important business aspects of your career on the basis that 'I just like being creative'. That's the difference between creativity as a career and creativity as a hobby." You will waste a great deal of time and money with this attitude, and it won't be apparent until both of these things are gone. If you are hoping a record label is going to pluck you from obscurity, stop wasting your time and educate yourself enough to be that person.

Believe it or not, there are a few people in this world whose dream it is to clean up your affairs while you write songs and have fun. Those who might hold those dreams would have to specifically like your music or piece of art and have the means to do what they say they can. In this instance, you find someone whose dream it is to boost your career by looking after your affairs, and you respect them and work closely with them rather than just leaving it all up to them! Otherwise, should anything happen, you'll be stuck with a career you never learned to manage yourself. This phenomenon is prevalent in the South African creative and broadcast industry. Most creatives are painfully dependent on agents and managers to handle their business affairs and are always found wanting when those who manage their affairs screw them or leave them for greener pastures.

Hence, I advocate for institutions of higher learning to make a deliberate attempt at introducing compulsory entrepreneurship modules in all arts curriculums in order to empower future artists to be able to handle all aspects of their creative business, and curb the rampant exploitation and abuse they may continuously suffer at the hands of those who see them as disposable idiots when no longer relevant. The South African creative arts industry, alongside the media broadcast industry, is a relatively small market where everyone knows everyone. Therefore, it's imperative for creatives to stay involved, connected, and friendly across all pursuits, or, as Skotty says, "Don't be a dick … I repeat … don't be a dick".

The behind you are kicking today *will* be the behind you are kissing tomorrow. Being easy to be around is just as much of an advantage in this business as being talented. Be a person of your word and maintain an upbeat optimism, even if it's only a business strategy. A good vibe in and of itself spreads and returns opportunities tenfold. Remember names and don't stuff around—everybody wants to hear their name, as it personalises the relationship. The more you screw people around by turning up late or acting like a diva, the less seriously they will take you.

The misconception usually peddled in the creative arts industry is that one doesn't need an education in order to make it, and when you dig deeper into the statistics of this theory, it is overwhelmingly shocking to realise how small the percentage is of artists and creatives that actually made it big without any formal training in the art or business of their chosen discipline. There is always a method to the madness. I never discard the importance of education, regardless of the sector you belong to and even in response to those who argue that you don't need an education to survive in the creative arts industry, particularly in music and, to a lesser degree, acting. As fair as this might sound, I wonder if they have taken some time to figure out who has been exploiting the creatives and what levels of education or training they hold.

More often than not, the 'middleman' is skilled, experienced, and well educated. It is no surprise that the people who speak ill of the importance of education and training are usually those who don't have it, and these are the ones who coincidentally end up being exploited and discarded with no tangible options following the failure of their artistic endeavour or 'one-hit wonder'. What most people often miss about formal training or education is that when things are not playing out the way you wanted or planned, education equips you with analytical skills and tools to survey the changing market conditions, and it allows you to pivot a new sigmoid curve in order to leapfrog from either competitive disadvantage or competitive party into a sustained competitive advantage for your own profit maximisation.

So many times, I have listened to people talk about billionaires who dropped out of school and are doing just fine, yet I never hear the conversation going a little bit further to interrogate who is actually running, growing, strategising, and sustaining those multi-billion dollar 'middleman' enterprises, and what level of education, skills, experience, and academic credentials they possess. If the theory of the invalidity of education and training to obtain success were to stand, these dropout billionaires would be hiring other dropouts just like them to run their businesses and pivot them to the greater heights they are at today. But they don't, and no one dares ask why. Economies have always been built on the backdrop of scientific research, innovation, creativity, hard work, and hunger to evolve and better the human species both socially and commercially; hence, I argue that anything outside of that is nothing but pure luck, coincidence, or the invisible hand of corruption and cronyism. I dare say that creative artists of all disciplines need to empower themselves with enough requisite skills to be comfortable with the idea that they *are* the business; they are the owners of technology that distributes their craft and software programmes that help them track their performance and royalties.

For as long as all these responsibilities are delegated to the 'middleman' and creatives absolve themselves from the discourse under the pretence that they want to focus on their passion and calling, the 'middleman' will continue to loot, exploit, and abuse them unabatedly and without flinching. The categories of exploitation, particularly in the music industry, are said to be divided in three ways: a) The inability of the creatives to own their masters or intellectual property; b) Creative artists entering into agreements that compel them to sign what are known as '360-degree deals'; and c) Creative artists entering into deals known as 'recoupment of cost' deals.

These are the types of deals that have placed the majority of artists in situations where they end up broke and broken, despite the sales revenue growth accruing from their creative productions. Instead, they end up owing the 'middleman' money they never thought they owed, a phenomenon that Dejo Andersson, CEO and founder of Eleven B Studios, labels as, "Horror stories of survivors of the music industry abound". He also argues that, "Everywhere we look, it seems like new artists are having stars put in their eyes only to have them ripped away soon after. An evil practice of the 'middleman' that leaves people with more questions than answers, trying to figure out 'What the hell is happening?' 'What's the cause of this seemingly scandalous behaviour?' A million-dollar question to a well-organised, oiled machinery that seems to make up every big record label across the globe. Attracting ambitious artists with irresistible promises of fame and fortune while conveniently forgetting to mention that they'll be lining their own pockets."

Going back to how these deals were established in the first place, it is said that once upon a time, there used to be a symbiotic relationship between the 'majors' and their signed artists. A "you scratch my back and I scratch yours" deal; a deal that decided that eighty-five percent of profits from a single release or album would go directly to the record label while the artists were free to do what they wanted with their fifteen-percent share. Although it worked, this is a deal structure that appears unfair at a glance, especially given that artists had full rights over profits accrued from touring, merchandise, and any financial gains or proceeds made independent of the record label. This was an era where the rosy picture of the record labels emanated from a situation where iconic and legendary artists were incredibly famous and rich, displaying an epitome of incredible success where record labels were only mentioned in terms of reverence and record deals sought after tirelessly by everyone who wanted to enter the game.

However, markets evolved and new technologies invaded the industry, while the competition began to intensify. Likewise, with the music industry, technology improved, and new on-demand music streaming subscription platforms erupted in the form of Rhapsody in the beginning and later Spotify, Soundcloud, and YouTube to name a few—a game-changing trajectory that saw the demise of CDs and physical albums, especially with the growth of internet access that enabled this market pivot to flourish, resulting in unprecedented sales drops and the record labels suffering losses and market share declines. This was a negative market trajectory that forced music business entities to change strategies and find ways to stay afloat; hence, the new developments and introduction of album advances and recoupable advances were a logical stunt to keep the 'majors' going. Andersson argues that album advances are probably the biggest and the most noticeable loophole in the system, where at the beginning, your new favourite artist would look like they have money to burn, showing off their luxurious lifestyle on social media—a 'bling-bling' type of lifestyle complete with gold chains, flashy cars, designer clothes, and expensive champagne. The type of lifestyle seen at KONKA establishments every weekend—balling with politicians and 'tenderpreneurs', forever surrounded by an entourage of half-naked young girls that are often classified as 'slay queens' and labelled 'yellow bone' based on their skin pigmentation. They look like they have made it, whereas that is the record label's money they are spending. As silly and frivolous as it appears, again I dare say, "This is nothing personal, it's a behaviour that has always been classified as just business."

The genesis of it all is that record labels know creative artists generally lack resources and, therefore, can own neither the production nor distribution means. Generally, recording any piece of music is quite expensive, and a lot of money is needed to get off the ground and make an artist or album successful. In addition to financial requirements, the following is also required: state-of-the-art recording equipment, writers, producers, engineers, advertising, promotion, *payola*, etc., so it does not come cheap, and this is all compounded with the artists' demands to stay in luxurious apartments or houses in upmarket neighbourhoods, even before revenue comes in. Before a hit song is even made or released, the record label incurs all the risks and financial cost of this lifestyle, and it knows how fickle the industry is and how the appearance of wealth and a lavish lifestyle fascinates the entertainment market and those watching from the outside. A strategy that ensures the artist will definitely attract fans, and the more fans an artist has, the more money the record label will make. However, there is no such thing as free lunch; all that money has to be paid back to the label, as it is considered a "recoupable payout". The payments are usually made from the fifteen-percent cut of the profits given to the artist.

To simplify the scenario and put things into perspective through a real-life example, for a new artist releasing their first album, the album will likely bring in R1 million on average, some making even less. However, R850 000 of this profit will go to the record label, leaving the artist with only R150 000—a deal that doesn't sound too bad until you factor in the album advance of R300 000, which would essentially leave the artist R150 000 in debt to the record label before they are even really famous or have released a hit song/album. Without a doubt, they can make that money back easily if they hit it big, but this is unfortunately rare and can leave the artist in a state of what I regard as modern-day 'slavery'.

What that means then is that, now that the artist owes the record label money, they have a compelling motive to create a new album. This is a practice that is usually done anyway in accordance with the contract they've already signed, except now there is more unintended pressure than ever before to make that money back—a scenario I equate to making a deal with the devil or signing your soul away. In some cases, the artist only realises at this point that the luxurious apartments and flashy cars that were bought at the beginning were in the record label's name. Now, there is suddenly the risk of losing it all if the artist doesn't comply with the record label in repaying the money or releasing the requisite album to repay the debt.

In extreme cases, some artists discover at this stage that even the household name they've been calling themselves, and which has been embraced by millions of fans, belongs to the record label too. And when they eventually manage to repay the debt and seek to release themselves from the record label in pursuit of their independence, they get the shock of their lives when they discover that they are not even allowed to use the stage/brand name they've been using and by which they are known by both media and the fans. The drama even escalates to their social media platforms that they've built over a long period of time into a verified multi-million-follower status, where these accounts now have to be deactivated as they too are classified as company assets, so if the artist wants to retain them, they would have to buy them back for ridiculous amounts of money.

Another strategy employed by the 'middleman' in the music industry is what is known as 'venture capitalism'—a strategy where the record label signs contracts with hundreds, if not thousands, of artists (depending on the resource size of the 'boogeyman') with the hope that one of these musical hopefuls will achieve the desired success. Even in the acting business or performing arts agencies, this is a familiar scenario in which hundreds of actors are signed up to be sent to auditions with the hope that one will land a spot in that big international movie contract, soapie, or *telenovela* that will give the agency positive cash flow. However, in reality, most of the artists remain struggling 'B-listers' that end up suffering from depression and never make it big into the Hollywood status they thought they would achieve.

At the core of creative artists' problems is the fact that too many people are involved in the production value chain, especially when it comes to the song-making process. Hence, the record labels make themselves demigods that know what works and what the public would like, and they market it aggressively to ensure optimal returns in the form of income; they peddle the idea that creatives can't be trusted to do this and also deliver professionally. This is exactly where artists lose control of the creative process, meaning that they have little influence on how the product is produced, which in turn enables a scenario where the 'middleman' gets to claim their masters/intellectual property and ensure that artists have no legal right over what is supposed to be their own creation. From a music industry perspective, a music master is essentially the final product, including the income it's projected to make in the future. How ridiculous is such a deal? This doesn't make sense! I can't even comprehend how artists get themselves into deals like this. The 'middlemen' have been screwing over many of their signed professional artists for decades now, claiming the bulk of the artists' profits and issuing them exorbitant loans knowing full well that the artists could never repay them.

It's a scenario that is no different from the Chinese, French, English, American, and German governments that come to Africa to offer substantial loans disguised as Foreign Direct Investments (FDI) in exchange for cheap labour, only to then take over key strategic assets of the country should it be unable to repay the loan. I assert that perhaps the 'majors' are deliberately and intentionally trapping artists in evil contracts that remove them from the production room—a strategic system that relegates artists to only perform on stage and record in the studio and nowhere else, while royalty-collecting agencies and digital streaming platforms alike are also short-changing the artists of their royalties and streaming percentage revenue split.

Given these circumstances, it is not surprising to witness that most people working in the creative arts industries face several challenges related to their overall mental health and well-being. The mere fact that there is no correlation between how talented you are as an artist and how successful you can be is enough to drive these creatives to the psychiatric ward. All creatives, regardless of the art discipline they are in, put their work out there to be judged, and it is even more challenging because they are not just judged or evaluated on their creative talents alone. It's about the scene they are in, what they look like, and what record labels and production houses they are part of—a very destructive environment that is enough to breed the types of 'crazy people' these creatives are perceived to be.

Creative professionals need to shift away from the notion that there is something wrong with being an artist that also wants financial success, for this is a belief system that impoverishes them while opening the gap for the capitalist 'middleman' to pounce and plug in the gap at their expense. I have often heard artists say, "A true artist only plays because he or she loves it, not for money," or "You shouldn't be concerned about making money; you should only be concerned about producing your art." My personal favourite is when artists proudly say, "Money should never be the motivating factor for an artist." These are self-inflicted shackles of poverty designed to make the artists' struggles appear cool and attractive and almost romanticise it as a credential of being a true and legitimate artist. This is a load of crap, in my view. I remember my orientation lecturer as a first-year Bachelor of Arts student at Nelson Mandela Metropolitan University lamenting that, "All those in this class hoping that they will be rich and famous upon graduating are in the wrong course, and you might as well change to another course now." Almost conditioning us from day one that we were entering a predetermined journey of suffering, struggle, and poverty where all that matters is passion, advocacy, and self-expression through the arts.

Like any other business, creative art is a product and a service sold to customers at a predetermined price, so why is that reality downplayed and veiled from the artists to fool them into believing they are following a bigger calling of spirituality, as long as they make audiences happy and bring joy and escapism for them through their artistic prowess? This is the nonsense that needs to come to an end. Since when is it a sin to want to be paid for the artistic skills you produce? Why is it okay to be recognised as a creative artist only when you are starving? Which other industry in the world applauds and celebrates someone for selling a product or service without expecting any reward in return?

Creative artists have been surrounded by the ignoramus commentary about this foolishness for so many years. Once again, artists need to learn about business and acquire entrepreneurial skills that are aligned to the arts discipline they specialise in. Everybody knows that learning about business, let alone the creative arts business, is work. Vultures know that artists don't want to do that work; they simply want to play, have fun, and get paid. Yet, they continue to remain poor. I sometimes can't help but feel that artists suffer from low self-esteem and derive their self-worth from the feedback they receive from fans rather than from their inner satisfaction and understanding of their worth as artists. Creatives should never feel bad or guilty for fighting or voicing out what they believe is injustice. The era of the 'middleman' is coming to an end, thanks to the internet and digital transformation. Across most industries, the 'middleman' has never been an expert producer of product or service; their core business has always been premised on moving the goods and services from the producer/supplier to the consumer.

This is a reality that confirms that none of the markets or enterprises could survive without the creatives or suppliers, as they are dependent on them for selling anything to begin with. Evidence beyond reasonable doubt that the real power still remains with the creative supply side of the equation and the customer demand side of the equation, and anything in the middle is nothing but a sophisticated, legalised scam pretending to make things easier, faster, and more efficient for the consumers to access. If creatives could only realise that and capitalise on the technological discontinuities and the universality of the internet to distribute, market, and sell their own product directly to the consumers, it would be the beginning of their power shift straight to being the originators of the product or service being supplied and cutting the 'middleman' out once and for all.

The veiled reality the creatives are perhaps never exposed to is the fact that the 'middleman' never had the skills, resources, or capabilities to produce the products film and television production houses supply nor the music the musicians produce; hence, their job is to use their financial resource to acquire the best the market can offer and use that to compete with other 'middlemen' for the domination of audience ratings, record sales, and the command of their attention. A lucky streak of dominance enabled by the broadcast networks' path dependency that has roots traced to government relations on both public- and private-owned enterprises.

3

THE SUPPLIER

While the previous chapters focused on the well-documented outcry of creative artists being exploited, abused, and dying as paupers with mostly nothing to show for their work in the hands of the supplying production companies, this chapter instead places emphasis on a purported veiled form of exploitation and abuse that is faced by the supplying production companies themselves in the hands of distribution enterprises. A hidden reality that manifests itself in every sphere of the media and creative arts value chain.

Accordingly, it is common knowledge that a supplier is an entity that provides goods and services to another organisation for trading and distribution to a large population of consumers. In an attempt to narrow the discussion to the creative arts and media broadcast industry, this chapter will focus on film and television production house enterprises as a subject of supplier discussion. Film and television production houses are creative and technical enterprises that are often small startups frequently accused of being semi-professional, and are sometimes purported to be just as dysfunctional and disorganised as the creative talent they employ.

These are institutions of creative output that are mostly established by creative professionals who got tired of accepting slave wages for their skills at the employ of the 'middleman' (in exchange for eight hours of work and a predictable salary) and decided to chase the creative bug of uncertainty, leaving out the 'middleman' in pursuit of entrepreneurial independence to tell their own stories and supply content to the same 'middleman' they once worked for, being the broadcast networks and over-the-top (OTT) platforms. Also included here are former creative artists who got tired of living from hand to mouth and subjecting themselves to the proverbial lottery of auditions at the mercy of the production houses. Essentially, they are group of talented individuals that finally smelled the coffee and decided to join the club of 'crazy ones' by forming their own production houses in order to compete for commissioning deals and potential funding opportunities, thereby joining a long list of creative businesses that are grounded in conceptualising, producing, and/or developing audio-visual content for broadcast television networks, cinemas, and online streaming platforms, to name a few.

What I've described here is a unique sub-sector of the electronic media economy that not so many people know about, except for film and television industry insiders. From a distance, this is an enticing type of business that may promise creatives all the purported glitz and glamour of the industry without going through the 'middleman'. However, upon closer inspection, it is really a business characterised by labour intensity yielding very little to no financial returns, unless you are a corrupt and bribery-prone executive producer, and it is a subsector with a romanticised reality of hustling and bustling that most creative executive producers are silent about. To summarise, this type of business is a façade of an industry plagued with extremely high levels of immorality wherein deep, tightened, and concentrated relationships are found at the top levels, with a handful of oligopolistic broadcast networks dependent on film and television production houses for audio-visual content productions to further their bottom line.

In this 'winner-takes-all' type of industry, the primary indicator of success is the number of commissioning deals you can clinch, especially for soapies or *telenovelas*. This is the epitome of competitive advantage that is derived from the economies of scale, as this type of commissioning deal constitutes a delivery of 260 episodes per year. A manufactured and desired level of entrepreneurial comfort most film and television production houses wish for, as it guarantees the production house sustained, year-round cash flow. Any production house operating outside of these parameters falls into the category of a struggling enterprise that does just enough to keep its lights on and maintains a status of competitive parity at best while squeezing its workforce to the bone, with some resorting to joining an even more proverbial quest for government grants and Presidential Employment Stimulus Program (PESP) stipends just to be able to produce a proof of concept (i.e., a pilot).

The opportunity for these types of grants plays a significant role in pacifying production houses who have largely given up on the idea of obtaining commissioning deals from the 'middleman' due to reasons spanning from the legitimate inferiority of their proposals to misalignment of their ideas with the broadcaster's brand strategic positioning or target audience. However, this does not negate allegations of the toxic gatekeeping of commission deals based on corrupt relations between commissioning editors, program managers, and production houses, which is another dimension of the conversation that most production houses would like to pretend doesn't exist in fear of exclusion, isolation, or victimisation by the broadcast networks. Funnily enough, this is a similar behavioural pattern that is, in turn, witnessed by creative artists and media practitioners on a daily basis at the hands of production houses.

The prevalent corruption/gatekeeping allegations in the industry make most sceptics like me believe that any production house that tries to convince you there are no corrupt relations between them and broadcast networks—and tries to sell you the narrative of a newly-found desire to promote new ideas, tell different stories, and unearth new voices—is either delusional or a beneficiary of the same broken and corrupt system. Hence, government grants and audio-visual funding subsidies (however small they are) have become an alternative option for most production houses to be able to tell their own stories in the absence of broadcast networks coming to the party and to genuinely open the industry for legitimate conceptual stories. This has become an interesting strategy for entering the industry, where some producers target these grants and state funding opportunities as a sole source of income to be able to produce something or at least have a proof of concept.

However, this is also just another broken system that fails more than it succeeds (if the measure of success is the entrepreneurial sustainability of the production houses funded), as the rate of rejections is just as high as the rate of submissions received by these funding agencies, which is a phenomenon that can, again, be explained by a number of reasons including the inferiority of the concepts submitted, non-compliance, and the lack of substantive evidence on the contribution the project will make in the community.

Be that as it may, the moral of the story is that the industry is broken, with some film and television production houses being at the centre of it all and others being at the receiving end of this brokenness. Success in this industry is predominantly based on *who* you know more so than *what* you know or what you can produce, which is an indication of a market failure by any measure, where bureaucrats and political hyenas reign supreme under the auspice of the "it's our time to eat" syndrome. You will never find creative artists occupying positions of power here wherein they can influence the strategic direction of the industry. Instead, they are relegated to being nothing but social media influencers endorsing politicians during the electioneering period.

The heavy reliance on a handful of broadcast networks to get business in South Africa is a calamity and a source of dysfunction, corruption, and exclusion of the majority of black creative producers in the country. A discussion that not only requires more broadcast networks to enter and disrupt this oligopolistic market, but also requires film and television production houses to be more intentional about their independence and financial freedom, and requires them to invest in establishing their own distribution channels to sell their content directly to consumers and cut out the infested dominance of the 'middleman' that serves no one but the corrupt gate-keepers in its employ.

One can never avoid the fact that within the same creative arts industry, some production houses earn relatively well amid the poverty and starvation outlined in earlier chapters, with trade deals that exceed those of other industries, depending on which side of the corruption pendulum you swing. However, contrary to popular belief, evidence indicates that the average income levels among production houses is comparatively lower than in most other industries, a phenomenon that suggests that taking up art as a profession/business is a suicide attempt. Hence, any deal that is less than a daily screen offering to the market is nothing but a slog and almost a hand-to-mouth type of business operation that barely breaks even and results in executive producers making zero return on investment on the production.

How this works is that, as an executive producer or production house, the expectation is that you get your share from the ten percent mark-up the broadcaster expects you to take as your dividend at the end of the production. Now, the hope is that you won't have too many partners in the company that will expect a share of these dividends—a business practice that requires a production house to have a strong, tough negotiator and a no-nonsense type of line producer that will ensure all production departments stick to the budgets and can get the best for nothing. This becomes a domino effect that cascades down to the rest of the business and is mostly construed as the exploitation of technical crews and creative talents (artists). Whereas the executive producers are faced with the challenge of maximising whatever they have within the time frames they have by ensuring the following:

• They clap as many scenes as possible in one day to ensure savings on production costs at the end of the production.

• They reduce the call fees to a bare minimum to ensure that there is some form of profitability at the end of the production. (Why bother getting into this business if there is no profit to be made?)

• They keep the talent fresh/new and inexperienced to maintain the lowest rates possible, with the hope that they can be trained and developed on set.

• They integrate influencers into the show at the request of the broadcast network for marketing and traction purposes.

This is a standard business practice with nothing untoward about it, unless it compromises the quality and production value of the content being produced for the client (i.e., the broadcast network). In any business, to remain in business and be able to yield some level of profit from your commercial efforts, it is always in your best interest to ensure that inputs are acquired at the lowest possible cost so that outputs can be sold at the highest possible price for revenue generation. Otherwise, the company is just wasting its time and running a charity organisation, and it is no different with production houses.

The aim is to get talent, crew, management, and resources to produce at the lowest *cost* possible in order to deliver the required content at the quickest *pace* possible for the purpose of selling to the broadcasters at the highest *price* possible, with the hope to deliver the highest production quality you possibly can. If this isn't achieved, these businesses would cease to exist, and the entire effort of establishing a production company would be a meaningless endeavour. It's important for creative artists to familiarise themselves with the whole ecosystem and understand how things work in relation to the commercial aspects of the creative arts business and how that affects their bottom line. It is, indeed, a very difficult balancing act that film and television production houses are faced with while dealing with the broadcast network contracts that are not favourable to them and are designed to serve the 'middleman's' bottom line.

Not so long ago, in August 2022, one of the country's most popular weekly newspapers, the *Sunday World*, published a piece focused on actors who wrote on social media platforms about how they were struggling to survive and were at a point where they could barely pay for their transport to work due to the precarity of their earnings, which amounted to the value of approximately R350 per call. For instance, one of the actors from a popular soapie cried and vented about how much of an 'A-list' talent she is and how she appears on national television almost every day with a perceived celebrity status, yet she earns as little as R6 000 per month, a despicable figure for a lead actor who is on set and on screen every single day of the week. "Do you know how humiliating it is to take a taxi with people who recognise you on screen, take pictures of you to circulate on social media because you can't even buy yourself a second-hand, entry-level car to go to work?" asked the actress, attributing all her challenges to the ruthlessness of the production house she was working for.

This is one of many examples of artists (both on screen and behind the scenes) that complain about how unsavoury the working conditions are for a cast or crew member employed by a local production house, a phenomenon that is indicative of how easily disposable artists are perceived to be in the media and creative arts industry regardless of the discipline they choose. The irony is that these are the same circumstances production houses cry about when complaining about the broadcast networks and how unsavoury the working conditions are between them, regardless of the acquisition model you choose to look into. A silent tug of war between the 'middleman' gatekeepers and the production houses, where executive producers complain about how junior and inexperienced commissioning editors are these days and how clueless they are about the business. Meanwhile, commissioning editors and program managers from the broadcast networks are, in turn, complaining about how clueless and inferior the quality of work is coming out of the content production industry.

This is a phenomenon that I believe could be the reason for the recent trend of closed pitches and preferential procurement of content that has developed quite rapidly in the film and television industry under the pretence of preserving quality and mitigating risk against 'newbies' and inexperienced producers. A loophole I argue is the root cause of dysfunction and corrupt tendencies permeating this industry, and one that raises rhetorical questions about how most of the existing production houses survive this mayhem. The systematic and cartel-like nature of the industry ensures that big projects—in the form of *telenovelas* and soapies—circulate among the same non-creative production companies that benefit from preferential procurement and closed (exclusive) pitching sessions. This is a precarious business practice that purports to be recognising experience over creativity and conceptual ideation, suggesting that as a start-up production company, you stand no chance of entering this market, let alone competing in it, regardless of how conceptually superior your production house might be.

It matters less in this industry how long you have been in the game as a professional. The purported narrative peddled for administrative purposes is that you still don't have the experience as a company that can deliver for the broadcast network, so until you do, it's always "Don't call us, we'll call you." At best, and if you are lucky, you are most likely to be partnered with a so-called 'seasoned' production company (that is already in the broadcaster's books or working within their network) that will be identified and recommended as a supervising entity for you in order to mitigate the risk of inexperience and to ensure micro-management of your project from beginning to end. A practice that goes as far as cash flowing your operations monthly to ensure delivery and identification of certain critical skills the broadcaster prefers you to work with, which include Head Writers, Directors, Line Producers, Show Runners, and key talent to be cast for brand alignment and marketing purposes.

As a result of this type of business model, by the time the project is finished, the producer might not even recognise the concept they initially envisioned. But because most producers are hungry and eager to build a profile for their production house businesses, and because they want to position themselves as credible filmmakers and television content producers, they toe the line and succumb to this ecosystem that doesn't necessarily benefit them but rather just keeps them afloat for a few months as long as they comply. Furthermore, if you manage to clinch a commissioning deal, that means that, as a production house, you also relinquish the show's intellectual property to the 'middleman' to exploit the content as much as it sees fit through its planned strategic repeats, foreign language dubbing, and licensing opportunities to other market territories or platforms. Again, this is a common practice in the industry that is applied across the globe; except perhaps the degrees of negotiation differ and are less exploitative internationally than they are here in South Africa.

As exploitative as this might sound, it remains a sound, orthodox strategy that ensures the broadcaster mitigates its risks and can guarantee that each piece of content they invest in will be delivered on time, on budget, and at a quality the 'middleman' desires. Broadcasters have been burned a number of times before, where production houses disappear without a trace upon getting the contract signed and receiving payments and never deliver the content that is required for the transmission (TX). Instead, executive producers are witnessed a few months down the line purchasing new SUVs and sports cars and enjoying holidays in exotic islands without having delivered the contracted content for broadcast or paying the cast and crew they worked with.

This has been a rude awakening for most broadcast networks that has culminated in revised business models wherein production houses are now forced to be cash flowed upon signing the contract and must have paid their pre-production and production money in trenches to ensure the completion of the project and delivery for the set TX dates. However, also bear in mind that if this is a commission, the show's intellectual property belongs to the broadcaster, and they can do as they please to exploit the asset to recoup their commissioning investment. A classic form of glorified slavery where the production houses operate as employees of the broadcasters to manage the production operations on the broadcaster's behalf for a concept that they originated.

The nature of this kind of trade deal means that the production house barely owns the means of production and relinquishes their conceptual assets to the one who pays for the commission (the 'middleman'). These are nuanced tribulations production houses face that perhaps creative artists are not aware of and/or perhaps don't even care to know, as long as their own bottom line is fulfilled. A conundrum that opens up unintended tensions in the industry, and evidence of how nuanced these issues are.

Everyone has their own struggles. If it takes three to ten years for some production houses to get one show on screen, the pertinent question is, "What was that production house surviving on for all those years?" Every now and again, I witness new companies breaking through the purported high barriers of entry with mediocre concepts, leaving everyone wondering how it happened. One cannot help but conclude that the system is rigged, as it's almost impossible to succeed unless you know the right people in the right places and are prepared to have 'adult conversations' with the gatekeepers on what gets commissioned and what doesn't, with the adult conversations being, "You scratch my back, I scratch yours."

On paper, the industry appears to be flourishing and contributing significantly to the country's gross domestic product (GDP). With the prospect of more foreign broadcasters entering the South African market, it seems that more opportunities for fresh content will emerge at face value. However, what most people don't understand is that it is a waste of time for production houses entering the market to submit their proposals to these establishments, as the narrative and voices will always remain the same while purporting the idea of diversity and inclusivity. A few weeks ago, I bumped into a content producer who mentioned that he had submitted and circulated more than 300 concepts across all broadcast platforms in the past eighteen months and yet hadn't received a single letter of intent or interest, let alone an invite to a pitching session.

His was an interesting utterance that made me wonder how mediocre this producer's concepts would be for him to be rejected or ignored 300 times in the space of eighteen months. He is a graduate from one of the most prestigious film schools in the United States of America and has more than eight years of experience, yet he received the cold shoulder 300 times. Surely something must be wrong here. For a minute, I felt like a spoilt brat and a whining baby for complaining about receiving just twenty rejection letters in six months of submitting to industry buyers and broadcast networks.

Then again, I realised that, as production houses, we are brainwashed to believe that our entrepreneurial survival is dependent on this handful of oligopolistic broadcast networks. The only way the technical crews and creative talent can begin to realise their real financial freedom is when production houses themselves realise their true worth and entrepreneurial potential independent of the traditional establishments, and when they begin to develop their own platforms and distribution channels that can help them trade directly with consumers at a smaller scale and affordable prices. It simply cannot be normal for a company to be pitching and presenting proposals for a duration of ten years and still have nothing to show for it. Clearly something is off.

Similar to the arguments I made in earlier chapters about artists knowing their worth, taking back their power, and making a concentrated effort to own the production and distribution means, production houses need to do the same and cut out the 'middleman' completely. That is the only time production house enterprises can begin to see the fruits of their creative and artistic labour and break away from the exploitative capitalist shackles that bind them to the small cartels of the existing oligopolies. The notion of creative self-expression being presented to certain individuals who will then decide whether your concept is of artistic value or not is absolute nonsense. As much as we all know that the only currency production houses have is their ideas and concepts, it means nothing when you also don't have the *financial* resources to produce and sell to the networks. Hence, most production houses are lining up for their lunch and are at the mercy of the corrupt 'middleman' networks. A friend of mine based in Sweden once said, "People must stop calling themselves producers until they produce something," essentially saying that you are never a producer until you have the financial resources to produce something worth watching. Traditionally, production houses are subjected to different types of acquisition models by the broadcast networks. These include the following:

1. Commissioning – This is an acquisition business model where the broadcaster funds 100 percent of the project that is proposed, unsolicited, by the production company. The major benefit of this model is that the production house doesn't have to pay for the production; the broadcaster takes care of all the costs of developing and producing the acquired content. However, like any other business, and as I've mentioned before, there is no such thing as a free lunch. The broadcaster is not funding this project from the goodness of their heart. This transaction is only permissible on the condition that the broadcaster owns the intellectual property of your concept and can exploit it and do as they please with it in terms of commercialisation, strategically repeating and re-licensing it to other platforms for further revenue generation and with no further proceeds to the original creator of the concept (the production company). In addition, the broadcaster will assign a commissioning editor to project-manage the entire production and ensure that it is delivered on time and in accordance with the broadcaster's deliverables in terms of editorial direction, brand positioning, and strategic competitiveness.

These are all the broadcaster's business-related non-negotiables that might result in the original concept the producer envisioned being totally different from what was proposed in the initial stages of the submission. However, there is nothing untoward in this model. Like any other business, the one who pays the bills and absorbs the risks dictates the rules of engagement and, most importantly, takes the lion's share of the profit margins. It's a 'take it or leave it' situation; there is no negotiation required. As much as the production company might look like a glorified employee in this instance, a financially savvy producer can still make it big if they are the one of the lucky few that has a *telenovela* or a soapie, as the economies of scale are greater on these due to the duration of the series. Whereas when you are commissioned for a once-off, limited series or feature, you are nothing but a struggling artist that is living from hand to mouth, and the only way you can survive is to squeeze everyone working on your production to the bone to ensure that there is something you will earn at the end. Hence, it is also not a surprise to find actors or presenters who become producers and yet can't change the status quo. They find themselves in the drag race of a labour-intensive business model with little to no reserves or dividends to share among those working on the projects—a phenomenon that invariably results in allegations of exploitation and abuse of artists on set. Another interesting discussion that needs serious attention is that it makes no sense to have all these artists sign a contract with the production company but never contest or raise their remuneration issues upfront, resulting in them later walking away, mid-production, if they are not happy. In other words, you find artists who entered into contractual agreements with a production company on a fee that they were not happy with, only to protest halfway through the production and vent on social media platforms about how unhappy and screwed they were by the production houses. However, apart from the negatives outlined in this model, it remains the most sought-after acquisition model by producers, for it offers better costs per *mille* (CPMs) than other acquisition models.

2. Licences – This acquisition model is a straightforward one where the production house invests in the development and production of the project and merely offers a broadcast window period to the broadcast network or streaming platform at an agreed upon or negotiated fee. The only snag about this model is that the licence fees are often too low for the producer to recoup their investment in creating the project. The matrix some broadcasters use to price these licences is based on an estimated twenty-five percent of the total value of the project, had they been the ones commissioning it. Most production houses feel hard done by this system, especially when the same matrix is not applicable to content that is licenced internationally/from other territories beyond local markets, and when there is alleged to be no agreed-upon quantitative matrix to measure the value of what it should cost a broadcaster to acquire a piece of content outside the potential sales projections and the show's probability to break even or generate return on investment (ROI). Hence, the lower the acquisition cost, the higher the projected ROI the broadcaster might realise, and the higher the acquisition cost, the lower the projected ROI the broadcaster might realise. This is often a deal-breaker for broadcast networks that results in a lot of rejections of concepts and/or proposals from the production houses. A strategic management decision that sends a signal to the acquisition manager that the content being proposed is not commercially viable if it lands below the break-even point, regardless of its creative genius or artistic superiority. This means that the affected production house must devise alternative commercial plans to exploit the content, as they will never yield the desired recoupment of the investment initially made to produce it. Therefore, for some, the default setting becomes funding and grants from government institutions such as the National Film and Video Foundation (NFVF), the Department of Trade, Industry and Competition (DTIC), the Gauteng Film Commission (GFC), or the KwaZulu-Natal Film Commission.

3. Pre-sale – This acquisition model is somewhat of a funding matrix, where a producer or the production house has managed to raise at least eighty percent of the production funds required to finish the entire filming of the project and are short of the remaining twenty percent. These figures vary from broadcaster to broadcaster, but this captures the ballpark ethos of the model. The eighty percent secured by the producer could be a combination of many different sponsors or funders, including commercial brands or government agencies. The crux of the matter is that the broadcaster will look at the production house's proposed concept and ascertain if the programme aligns with the network or channel's strategy, channel schedule needs, and the channel's target audience, and is unique enough for them to invest in and go to market with. However, even if the concept ticks all the editorial and creative boxes for the broadcaster, similar to the license acquisition model, the ultimate litmus test is the revenue projection test. The cost of acquiring this content should yield a positive ROI, or at least break even. What is flawed about this measuring exercise is that the projections of the potential profitability of the proposed show are measured based on the historical performance of the proposed slot within which the show is earmarked to be scheduled—meaning there is no scientific proof or watertight evidence to substantiate how the show will perform from an audience or revenue standpoint, and suggesting that the new show is invariably at the mercy of how the previous show performed in the envisaged slot to project how well it will do in these areas. This is a fundamental decision that determines which show goes on screen and which one doesn't, and it is a common reality that means a lot of shows might not make it to the small screen despite having won the creative and editorial rigour test.

With this in mind, it's not a surprise to hear that there is a plethora of excellent shows that never saw the light of day on the small screen, shows that had all the ingredients to revolutionise the industry and push the creative boundaries of the country to unprecedented levels. There is still a benefit of this acquisition model though, which is that the production house still retains its intellectual property and is merely selling a licence window period for the broadcaster to sweat the property, which in turn allows the producer to continue distributing and licencing the asset to other platforms as they wish. However, what buys the broadcaster with its twenty-five percent investment is the editorial interference in the creative decisions around the storyline direction, casting, and look and feel, to name a few. This is also tricky because these broadcasters still want to effect some changes on the content to suit their brand. In contrast, as a producer, you still want to send this show elsewhere for consideration, which can be a deal-breaker for broadcasters and, in turn, a different form of screwing production houses. This is another scenario that demonstrates how important it is for the production houses to start cutting themselves loose from the 'middleman' and start developing their own platforms to trade directly with customers (the viewers) and sell their own advertising and subscription packages online. Similar to the creative artists, production houses are often squeezed by the 'boogeyman' to relinquish their power and subject themselves to a lot of exploitation and abuse in exchange for survival. A phenomenon that translates itself into a domino effect where they exercise the same abuse and exploitation to those they do business with (e.g., suppliers and talent), resulting in a dysfunctional system that is broken and brutally abusive. However, some do manage to escape the cycle by colluding with the 'middleman' gatekeepers and giving into the invisible hand that maintains the status quo.

4. AFP – This acquisition model is what we call Advertiser-Funded Programs, and is one I believe is by far the most lucrative of all the deals and an "I don't need your approval" type of model, where the broadcaster has little editorial influence on the content presented because it is sponsored by a commercial brand or product that doesn't require the broadcaster's money. It only needs a slot to buy, and a schedule to push its products. Broadcasters need the money; therefore, production houses selling the AFP are ninety percent more likely to get the show passed. However, the noticeable phenomenon about this acquisition model is that most production companies coming through with these proposals are white owned, but it's no surprise that this is the case. We all know that the advertising industry is still predominantly white owned, and it is made quite evident at times with how black people are sometimes represented in most of the commercials that we see on screen, even thirty years after the country's democratic dispensation. I don't think the advertising industry really understands the black consumer and what type of buying power they have.

For example, theoretically, in radio, the media buying matrix is centred on the footprint, reach, and number of eyeballs exposed to your communication regardless of your medium. If this is true, isn't it astonishing to realise that the biggest national radio stations in South Africa, such as Ukhozi, Umhlobo Wenene, and Metro FM, have been broadcasting for many years without fail while generating far less commercial sales revenue than the likes of 947, 702, and Jacaranda FM, which are regional radio stations with a fraction of the audiences the afore-mentioned stations deliver? This is a form of commercial racism that the market doesn't value, or the market just simply doesn't believe in black buying power. These numbers are almost treated as useless and as representing nothing but quantity with no quality that can be converted into monetary terms.

The same can be said about the production houses. Word on the street is that big-budget advertising campaigns are always awarded to white-owned production companies, whereas low-budget advertising campaigns are always awarded to black production houses regardless of size, experience, or skill set. An alleged conspiracy theory that also transcends to film and television production houses, where only white-owned production houses often get the opportunity to work with foreign Hollywood studios that are seeking local partnerships in the African continent for local stories. Some producers argue this to be a form of systemic racism no one wants to talk about in fear of isolation.

Although we've recently seen an emergence of more creative and flexible models of content acquisition across the globe, essentially these four are the basic ones at play and the primary decision-making processes production houses are confronted with, as well as the balancing acts they have to perform regularly. A veiled operational balancing act no producer ever talks about as they navigate their way to survive in the midst of creative artists and technical crews calling them greedy charlatans that enrich themselves on the back of their blood, sweat, and tears, and disregarding the fact that these are small creative businesses forever being hit with tough choices of deciding who to pay first between the rent of the premises they operate in and the artists contracted to deliver performances for the production.

Short-form production houses are the ones probably hit the hardest in this disaster of an industry, as these are production house entities that specialise in on-air campaigns for the broadcasters in the form of concept-themed pieces, generic promos, episodic promos, line-ups, on-air imaging, and events of national importance, including channel identity tool kits. Suppose you find yourself on a retainer contract—it is a better deal, as you can easily benefit from the economies of scale and manage to keep yourself afloat for a prolonged period of time, on the condition that the timeous delivery and conceptual superiority remain consistent.

However, the challenge with this type of specialisation is that it requires the entity to have some level of cash available upfront to put together the presentations for 'request for quote' (RFQ) submissions. This is a financial risk the production house absorbs from the get-go, without even knowing if they will get the job or not, and it is a supply chain management requirement I believe is designed to impede the new entrants in the market. It also makes no sense, as anyone can rent those skills required to ensure excellent delivery of quality campaigns that are aligned with the client's overarching strategy and creative objectives.

Therefore, the assertion is that perhaps this is nothing but a tactic to eliminate those that the 'middleman' does not want and instead open space for those it prefers for the procurement of the job, although this doesn't negate the fact that there are 'fly-by-night' production houses being hired that take chances and have no clue of the business, let alone the requisite skills, to deliver the job broadcast networks desire.

How many campaigns have you seen that are produced by the so-called 'seasoned and experienced' production houses and yet yielded no projected ROI, as the 'middleman' would like to make us believe? The bottom line is that the entire film and television industry is rigged and in the hands of the select few that own the production means and are in bed with the gatekeepers in the employ of the 'middleman'. A familiar practice that is prevalent in both the private and public sectors alike, but even more so at privately-owned platforms where draconian business practices are veiled and underplayed, with underpinnings that are traced back to the alleged demise of public broadcasting enterprises across the globe.

I don't blame them, though; it's a cut-throat industry where all players are competing for a small slice of the advertising pie. The film and television industry is a labour-intensive one that is very expensive to manage, let alone to win at. I have a profound admiration for people who embark on this type of business, as this indicates what people are prepared to endure to pursue what they consider their passion/calling, or for the love of creative arts. It's a whole different type of crazy where some people would decide to quit their day jobs to join this mayhem of content production in an insane industry. Theoretically, one would be inclined to think it'll be a walk in the park, until you realise that rejection is the name of the game. Just a getting a call to pitch a story to the broadcast networks is regarded as a miraculous act of God, and producers would be jumping for joy at the indication that they are on the right track. Some producers are even just grateful to receive any type of response, regardless of how negative or automated it might be.

Being a film and television production house in South Africa is an extreme sport where most are breathing through the pain and navigating a tough terrain that is enough to drive anyone crazy. Although it is easy for me to vent all these observations of how the industry's dysfunction operates, regardless of what sub-sector of the creative arts one belongs to, the industry is rotten to the core. Everyone is a casualty, and we all have a story to tell about how insane it is for anyone to continue chasing the façade of this so-called 'artistic dream' of authentic storytelling. But be that as it may, one thing that no one can take away from this industry, regardless of how broken it is, is that art will always have the magical power to change people's lives and turn them into better people. One of the remarkable attributes of the arts is the fact that it heals. Hence, I sometimes argue that art is equivalent to a modern-day form of religion, and it could never be too expensive for people to consume nor too inaccessible for the poor to enjoy, as that would be contrary to the notion of social justice.

The beauty and necessity of art is the driving force that brings me to highlight the importance of production houses taking matters into their own hands and using the power of the internet to produce and distribute content directly to the viewer, thereby cutting out the pandemic of an oligopoly in the name of a 'middleman' and legitimately democratising the industry for everyone to play and heal societies with their stories. Viewers don't care which platform you are on; all they care about is the content that you produce. If they like it, they will choose it and will be more likely to pay for it. Look at what podcast culture is doing to the credibility and authenticity of traditional radio as we know it—this is a new wave of creative self-expression that advertisers are also noticing and slowly placing some of their budgets on.

The film and television industry is no different. Production houses are probably the smallest yet some of the most powerful entities in the country. They possess the skills and power to break the shackles of the current exploitative, bureaucratic system controlled by the stale broadcast oligopolies. The era of asking for a seat at the table and banging on the already-sealed doors is over. This is the time and the era for production houses to create their own doors, sculpt their own tables, and forget about the lethargic institutions that are comfortable with recycling the same stories from the same non-creative, corrupt production houses that have been in existence since time immemorial. The advent of the internet has made things much easier and perhaps enables everyone who believes in themselves to dare take a chance and see what happens.

Production houses owning their production means and distribution platforms is not the magic wand that can 'un-screw' creative artists and media practitioners over-night; rather, it is the beginning of a prosperous industry free from the political economy and corrupt oligopolies driven by commissioning editors and program managers inside the 'middleman' ecosystem. It is the start of a new trajectory where the creative arts economy legitimately democratises itself and becomes a true market economy where the *consumer* is the one who decides what constitutes the best content, not the gatekeepers that reserve commissions and licences for their favourite (underperforming) production houses under the guise of closed pitches or preferential procurement processes masquerading as experience and institutional memory.

However, there is still something to be said about the principle of paying your dues. Just because the industry is rigged and those benefitting see nothing wrong with the status quo and myopically believe that everyone is given a chance, it doesn't mean that there is nothing to be said about the previously mentioned 'fly-by-night' production companies that don't possess creativity or innovation and never invest in their craft to push the splendour of high production value and creative pieces of work that shift the needle of the film and television industry to the next level, but instead just continue to submit torturous, sub-standard concepts that do not make sense even to five-year-olds.

Indeed, the theory of creativity is a discipline of subjectivity that doesn't help the discussion. Production houses need to invest in the up-skilling of their talent and development of concepts, alongside their business acumen, management, administration, and leadership skills. Being passionate and believing that you have a calling is not enough. The creative aspect of running a film and television production house as a business is the fun part (and probably the most insignificant part of it all). Paying more attention to the strategic and adminis-trative needs of the business is by far the most important factor and the one that can determine if you get a contract or not, and the one which can sustain you for much longer than the creative ideas could.

But the flip side of the coin also applies. Taking corruption and bribery conversations aside, there is also merit in broadcasters rejecting some of the ideas that come to pass for their consideration. The new market entrants need to prove they can deliver quality content that appeals to a large audience. These are the real scenarios in the industry; hence, it is justifiable for the broadcasters to resort to certain measures to protect themselves from such risks, wasteful expenditures, and irregular payments that often result in legal costs when chasing down production companies that can't deliver the contracted content. Commissioning every Tom, Dick, and Harry might not be a commercially viable decision for the broadcaster regardless of how good they look on paper, so betting on a tried and tested horse with a proven track record is also a reasonable decision any executive can make in order to save time and money.

All creatives believe that they have the best concepts and deserve a chance. But guess what? No one is thinking about that submission you made to the broadcaster. I have witnessed producers who submit an average of twenty proposals to different broadcasters monthly and are likely to only get one or two projects each year (if they are lucky). I guess what I am trying to say is that anyone dependent on this business for survival and hoping that they will very soon get a primetime soapie or *telenovela* slot is naïve and borderline delusional. Your best bet is probably to partner with whoever is already occupying the slot and pitch to them so that they can submit with you or on your behalf to the 'boogeyman', before you suffer from depression or wait for a commissioning deal that will never come. If you think this is too pessimistic, take a look at how many soapies and *telenovela* projects are occupying primetime slots across the landscape, evaluate how long they have been on screen, and notice which production houses have been delivering them, while also evaluating which relationships these production houses have in the broadcast network's hierarchy. Then tell me what you think.

The advent of the internet and the rapid growth of digital platforms have transformed the film and television industry, with unimaginable implications for strategies and tactics to fund audio-visual productions and exploit the economic value of the creative content produced by production houses. The emergence of video-on-demand (VOD) services and the technological changes for content distribution in the broadcast industry are enough to convince any production company that this is the direction to go in and is a new wave that needs to be embraced. A trajectory with the potential to liberate small businesses from the shackles of traditional networks' exclusion by instantaneously shifting audiences and financial powers away from the existing broadcasters, thereby allowing production houses to create their own lane, carve their own path, and explore the unprecedented opportunities that could prove to be far more profitable than begging the existing establishments for a seat at the table.

Many production houses and independent producers suffer from a lack of bargaining power in their negotiations with commissioning broadcasters, thereby creating a scenario where the attitude and posture of the broadcast networks is a 'take it or leave it' business transaction in which they alone dictate the value of the concept and what they are prepared to pay for it. This unconscious domino effect then leaves producers with no choice but to squeeze everyone they deal with in their value chain to ensure the attainment of their bottom line while plugging the hole left by the broadcasters during the negotiation tables.

Unlike markets such as the ones found in the UK and U.S., South African broadcasters have stagnated in the television production funding models mentioned previously and have resisted migrating to the more progressive models other countries have adopted to benefit the production houses. While commissioning terms vary from one individual to the next and from one country to another, the deals offered to production houses are generally designed to benefit the broadcaster more than the production houses, the majority of which are small, struggling businesses with no choice but to conform to whatever deal lands in their lap.

Some might contest the idea of production houses being screwed or exploited, as these companies are not held at gunpoint to be in this market or operate in this industry; they enter these deals knowing very well what they entail. So coming out at the tail end of the equation and crying 'foul' as their means to justify their unjust treatment and abuse of artists in general is therefore seen as unfair to the industry; the production companies should take accountability for its dysfunction as well. Regarding the retention and control of ownership and intellectual property for the production companies/houses, Professor Gillian Doyle—a well-established economist with special interest in media and cultural industries—laments that, in conjunction to these deals, production houses should produce effective exploitation of these assets depending on the windowing strategies employed by the producers or distributors.

The key difference between the local and European markets is that, unlike in Europe and the U.S., local production houses are subjected to windowing deals that see broadcasters as owners of the production means, in the sense that these broadcasters are granted a specific 'window period' during which they have exclusive access to the created content to exploit as they see fit, with the producers then only able to relicense the content to other broadcasters once the window period has elapsed. They also become the sole beneficiaries of online distribution windows for television content, such as online catch-up, Advertising-based Video on Demand (AVOD), Subscription Video on Demand (SVOD), and Transactional Video on Demand (TVOD) services. Invariably, production houses in South Africa are designed to operate from hand to mouth while the broadcasters are milking the residuals that come with the content produced by the production houses. Hence, it is no surprise to witness most production houses transferring these systematic shackles to the creative artists and technical crews they employ, creating a perpetual cycle of screwed creative personnel in a screwed creative arts industry.

Although OTT players have undoubtedly played a critical role in opening up and democratising the market, the most significant changes emanated from the proliferation of channels, Pay TV, satellite, and digital channels leading the windowing marketplace. In my view, in a country where the public broadcasting service is still the dominant player in terms of footprint and audience ratings (ARs), terrestrial broadcasting should be getting the first window period for slate availabilities and should be first to market licence distributions.

However, these broadcasters are still plagued with incompetence and bureaucracy that is premised on their outdated governance policies and processes, where business plans drafted for every content acquisition are circulated across multiple divisions for approval before negotiation can even begin with the suppliers (i.e., the distributors or content providers). This is a laborious manual process where administrative officials are subjected to drafting letters of intent or letters of purchase after already agreeing with the supplier on the deal, only to again circulate these letters to different divisions to sign off for final approval. All of this takes place before the contract can even be drafted, which is another process that can take three to six weeks before being sent to suppliers for input. Once the contracting process is finally complete, it may then turn out that the content acquired is no longer relevant for the market or has possibly already been snatched by the next competing broadcaster in the form of Pay TV or an OTT platform for a better fee. Hence, I argue that perhaps the demise of the public service 'middleman' is systematic and deliberately designed to allow the private one to gain monopoly, and any executive who wishes to transform a public organisation such as this into a lean, mean machine that is self-sufficient and competitive is doomed to fail.

Therefore, as easy as it is to blame film and television production houses for the exploitation of artists, it is worth noting that the biggest exploiter of the game is the man in the middle (i.e., the broadcast networks) who creates a domino effect which relegates film and TV production houses into nothing but glorified employees that are merely project-managing an audio-visual project on behalf of the broadcast networks with zero equity or ownership abilities. It is an entrenched hand-to-mouth system that is difficult to dismantle unless production houses become intentional about producing and distributing their own content with the objective to completely cut out the 'middleman' and sell directly to the consumer/viewer/streamer.

My view about the power of the 'middleman' in the broadcast industry is that the only time the fall of the 'middleman' is possible is when it implodes due to 'brain drain' that exits the enterprise (i.e. personnel that are skilled, qualified, and experienced), or when it suffers sabotage by its own staff compliment playing into the hand of other privately owned 'middlemen'—exhibit A being the state of state-owned enterprises (SOEs) across the African continent. Take, for example, the traditional linear broadcasting enterprises. All of them are failing dismally to transform themselves into dynamic enterprises that are self-sufficient and financially strong enough to fund their public service mandate, which is a failure and a market erosion I purport to be deliberate, not a mistake. I dare argue that this failure is a man-made machine intentionally designed to collapse the enterprises from within. A well-orchestrated implosion and dichotomy that is compounded by the long-historic debate of the paradox of servicing unfunded public mandate while being expected to deliver on the commercial interests of the enterprise. A tug of war that is enabled by all stakeholders involved, including the suppliers of this institution.

4

THE MIDDLEMAN

The 'man in the middle' is an entity that I argue was developed for the sole purpose of interfering with communication or manipulating transactions between people or enterprises. It is a phenomenon that I believe is equitable to a syndrome that can be classified as gatekeeping and cartel-like in orientation—greedy and heartless behavior complete with parasitic traits of a criminal gone corporate, or a broker gone rogue, if you like—and a phenomenon that is infested with a bunch of political hyenas and so-called 'captains of industry' that are masquerading as shape-shifters and social pioneers while sucking the blood of innocent consumers and poor citizens dry for profiteering purposes. The 'middleman' is a dominant force of evil that permeates all industries, including government agencies, state-owned enterprises, media conglomerates, political parties, and the education and health systems, to name just a few. It is no longer the noble concept that was, once upon a time, pundit to be for the ease of doing business and connecting suppliers with consumers, with the government playing a central role in creating an environment which enables this to happen in both public and private enterprises.

THE GOVERNMENT

The business model of the 'middleman' is one that adds and captures value between the producer and the consumer, and one that involves an intermediary moving goods and services from one party to another and facilitating transaction between the parties involved. The exception to this model, however, is the case of the government, where citizens play the role of suppliers and consumers of services through their taxes being deducted by the government ('middleman')—the only difference being that we never really receive the service we pay the government for. This conundrum has fueled so much anger among citizens and has resulted in some sections of society cutting this 'boogeyman' out and resorting to private sector services in order to access even the most basic services such as security, education, and healthcare. Some are even going as far as extracting themselves completely from the electricity grid by installing solar panels or investing in generators to power their houses and businesses, and others are making alternative plans to obtain water supply independent of the government.

These are the scenes that have been playing out in full view since the dawn of our democracy. South Africa was a capable state once full of dreams and enormous potential to be one of the most powerful shape-shifters coming out of the global south, but this has sadly become a dream deferred for a country that has quickly evolved into a shadow of its former self. A country that was to be a beacon of hope and a gateway to the African continent, and a country with a 'rainbow nation concept' that has since fizzled out along with the 'Nelson Mandela euphoria' of building a united, democratic nation where all are equal in front of the law and can live side by side in harmony regardless of race, age, class, gender, and cultural/religious beliefs. Not only have we dismally failed to make this dream a reality, but we have deviated from a vision of addressing inequalities among our citizens since the so-called 'new dawn', instead morphing into a 'gangster' state where the divide between rich and poor has grown ever faster and wider.

The government has not only failed to deliver a better life for all (as per the promises made to the masses in 1994) but has lied continuously to the poor who continue to live in abject poverty and with indignity. Our nation is in a state where even the middle class, who are purported to be the major drivers of the economy and were once promised an economy that would ease the burden off their shoulders, are relegated to the periphery while the looters are running rampant and destroying every state-owned entity this country has ever had. We are living in an economy that has since taken away from the middle class and delivered only to the 'middleman', otherwise known as the government.

Interestingly, sizeable populations of most countries continue to consider themselves as part of the middle-class society, if the income matrix is anything to go by, which is an assertion I suppose could also be the reason why the middle class dominates the rhetoric across the political spectrum. Yet few members of this middle-class population think of themselves as actually being part of the 'middleman' concept. I don't blame them ... I mean, why would anyone identify as the 'middleman' when the name itself carries a negative connotation and is deemed derogatory, with suggestions that the 'middleman' creates no value or, at best, is a necessary evil. Yet, while the government is indeed the evil, parasitic 'middleman' that adds no value, when taking a closer look at this 'middleman' concept, you realise that a huge number of middle-class people are also in 'middleman' professions, regardless of how much they want to avoid the word. Any profession that connects buyers with sellers, in my view, is a 'middleman' profession—for example, sales representatives, real estate agents, financial advisors, head -hunters, insurance brokers, etc. Furthermore, there are many other jobs in complex economies that have a less obvious 'middleman' component. Think of wedding planners—those stylish and ultra-organised women and men who orchestrate big events and help keep the bride from becoming bridezilla. That doesn't sound like a 'middleman' job, until you consider all the vendors (such as the florist, the baker, and the wedding-gown maker) that must be carefully selected and held to the highest standard of their professions. Lawyers, too, act as 'middlemen' when they broker deals. Your family doctor is a 'middleman' when he or she refers you to a specialist or, more often, prescribes one particular drug rather than another; if your health insurer is a 'middleman' between you and your doctor, your doctor is a 'middleman' between you and the drug maker.

The 'middleman' element in these types of jobs isn't always apparent to the person doing the work, but it can make the difference between doing a decent job and doing an excellent one. For jobs where the 'middleman' element is the very essence of the job, the effect of not playing the role well is even worse. Buyers and sellers have certain expectations of people in a 'middleman' position, and not meeting those expectations can sour business relationships (but people rarely express these expectations until things go wrong). However, be that as it may, and in accordance with the preceding chapters, this book will focus less on individual 'middlemen' and more on the 'middleman' as organisations, the government being one of these—an evil type of 'middleman' that is meant to facilitate activities and services of a country on behalf of its citizens at a price determined by taxes. Instead, this typical 'boogeyman' does what all 'middleman' organisations end up doing: loot the resources and exploit and abuse citizens unabatedly without shame or guilt. This is a pandemic I believe citizens have accepted and normalised for far too long in South Africa, and similar to previous chapters where I advocate for both creatives and film and television production houses to cut out the damn 'middleman', I dare say cut the damn government out too, and with the aid of new digital technologies, let the people govern.

As controversial as this might sound, out of all the 'middleman' institutions that occupy strategic spaces of the economy, I believe that the government is by far the most evil 'boogeyman' of them all—a 'boogeyman' with no conscience, and a devil who wears no shame in seeing commercial opportunities (even in the midst of the COVID-19 pandemic, for instance) for only itself and those connected to it to line up their pockets. The government is an evil enterprise that is happy to destroy the education system of the country just to keep the illiteracy levels of the population low enough to ensure the poor continue getting poorer and stay dependent on social services grants that are in themselves inadequate and insufficient for anyone to survive on.

This is a classic strategy of keeping the lower-class tier of the population out of the intellectual discourse surrounding the incompetence of the government, although the government is suddenly very competent when it has to deal with disgruntled citizens and eliminating them when they question its behaviour and are publicly vocal about its shenanigans. A classic state of calamity has transformed this once capable state into a dog-eat-dog world where it's survival of the fittest, and it has created a toxic environment where crime and murder rates are worse off than in war-torn countries, yet we are not even at war. South Africa has become a country unworthy of raising children in by any stretch of the imagination.

We are a severely weakened state that has collapsed beyond repair thanks to the 'boogeyman' in the name of government. A new economic order has fostered the prosperity and growth of private enterprises (that have plugged the gaps left by the state) to serve the public at a premium price, which is a phenomenon that sees private education, private security, private healthcare, and private transport systems raking in unimaginable profit margins never seen before in the history of our democracy, suggesting that perhaps the democratic dispensation this country entered into post-1994 is by far the best thing to have happened to the private sector in South Africa. Whereas, on the other side, it's the worst thing to have happened to the poor majority of the population and citizens of this country as a whole.

This conundrum raises further questions of conspiracy surrounding the invisible hand of the markets and how intentional and deliberate it is in ensuring the failure of this state, especially when the 'middleman' takes the form of government officials who, for their own enrichment, have shares in some of the private enterprises plugging the service delivery gap left by the government. Or, perhaps, the self-serving and corrupt inclination of political leaders is, on its own, the invisible hand that enables the shift of power away from the state and towards private enterprises to do the work that was meant to be done by the state. The private sector has thus become a new 'boogeyman' that appears at least more effective, skilled, efficient, and professional (depending on which side of the economy one resides), although at the same time is unaffordable for the poor masses and only accessible to those that can afford private services.

The crux of the matter is that if the dysfunction and collapse of the state ('middleman') is something that is prevalent in all sectors of the economy and has manifested itself at all levels of government, what do we think will happen to weaker, unregulated, and semi-professionalised industries such as the creative arts and media broadcasting industries? Not so long ago, the country stood witness to the creative arts industry, specifically musicians, marching to the Department of Arts and Culture agencies (e.g., the National Arts Council) and threatening to sleep in their offices, accusing them of mismanaging millions of rands worth of funds that were meant to be distributed to the music industry and deserving artists during the COVID-19 pandemic. The audacity of stealing these relief funds is indicative of a state that has lost its conscience and moral high ground, an evil 'boogeyman' of a different kind that is determined to burn this country and all its industries to the ground along with its citizens.

Take the public broadcasting service, for example. Another failed 'middleman' in the hands of the same evil government that, for the past decade, has been on a slippery slope of instability, uncertainty, insolvency, irrelevance, leadership crises, alleged political interference, and redundancy … the list goes on. It has become an institution that is no different from all other state-owned enterprises (SOEs) in the control of the government, a phenomenon that suggests the 'middleman' indeed always has the power, except the difference might lie in whose benefit this power is used for/on behalf of.

What I'm essentially saying is that the tone and energy of this country is set by the government, a type of 'middleman' that is meant to play a 'big brother' role in protecting its citizens and the sovereignty of the state and creating an environment that enables a better life for all who live in it, instead of playing the role of an evil 'boogeyman' that extorts tax from its citizens just to enrich itself and those in close proximity to political power. However, one can also argue that this is a self-inflicted pain of abuse in which, every five years, citizens have the opportunity to remove this 'boogeyman' of a government but choose to bring it back at any chance they get for further abuse and looting. A psychological behavior indicative of a traumatised society that doesn't value itself and is probably clueless of its own worth and what it deserves.

This scenario makes me wonder what things would be like if we could cut this 'middleman' government out, along with all the political parties, and vote directly for the individuals we wish to represent us and take care of the country's activities, using new technologies as a mechanism to do so. Or, better yet, what would it be like if we could remove the entire human element of running the affairs of the state and create a digital technology platform that can take care of them without human intervention or political manipulation? A new form of state control and service delivery where everything is digital and no political parties are required. An environment where the governing power of the state is truly democratic, technological, and shared among all citizens of the country and where all decisions are digitally transparent and managed via algorithms and tech systems powered by blockchain technology and impossible to hack. A digital state where artificial intelligence reigns supreme and everything is digitally available and accessible to all, in real time, at the click of a button.

This would include all state tenders that are advertised, at what value are they capped, which companies are in the race, what profile and experience they have, which companies the system selects, and which criteria the system uses to select the shortlisted and winning bidders, as well as all government-related jobs regardless of the level they occupy. This would be a system where citizens of the country could gain access to a database of all jobs/positions of any government department and SOE to see which position is advertised, for which department, what credentials were required, who applied for the jobs, who was shortlisted, and who got appointed. Corruption would be cut out instantly, and real democracy and power of the people could be a reality instead of the superficial power citizens are manipulated to believe they have today. Politicians are the biggest cancer the public has ever suffered against, and anyone who believes that a better life for all will come from them is either delusional or completely out of touch with reality (if they are not a beneficiary of this corrupt system themselves).

A DIGITAL GOVERNMENT IMAGINED

Imagine a state where the president and government ministers are digitally voted for by all citizens via a live technological platform, and the votes are based on skills, expertise, experience, and credentials without any political affiliation or parties. A digital system/platform that will be accessible to all citizens to see which minister is responsible for which projects in what department, what budget is allocated for that department and each project for the reporting year, and what timelines are assigned to each project for each minister. This would be a digital, nationwide technological platform that could be synchronised to any device of your choice and where you could log on to any province, city, village, or street and see in real time what is meant to be delivered, by who, when, how, and at what cost. A system that can be set to signal a red flag to every member of the population via their chosen devices when the deadline of any project hits and the project has not been delivered, and the public could then vote in real time and with immediate effect to remove the person tasked to deliver the project without waiting for the next general election to effect changes that never happen anyway.

This might sound like a 'pie in the sky' and an impossible task for a country with a track record of failing more than it succeeds. However, the optimist in me believes that, judging by the rate at which this country is deteriorating and the cost of living getting too high for anyone to keep up with, using data and technology to eliminate corruption and deliver efficient public services that meet citizens' expectations should be a priority, as it would cut out our toxic, incompetent government along with all these evil political parties that are serving no one but themselves. I especially believe this considering that market conditions have long embraced technology solutions and are rapidly changing at unprecedented speeds. Arnauld Bertrand, an EY Global Government and Public Sector Consulting Leader, and Julie McQueen articulate it better in their article titled, "How to build the digital state".

In their own words, it is argued that, as demand for public services grows, budgets tighten, and citizens become more empowered, "business as usual" is not an option for governments anymore. They need to rethink the way they deliver services to the public and harness new technologies to tackle national, regional, and local issues. In Africa, though, governments would rather think of ways to deliver services to their friends and families instead of to the public. It is common knowledge that new technologies can offer tremendous opportunities for governments to accelerate transformation, including how they themselves are elected or voted into positions.

Bertrand and McQueen further assert that when technology is used as a strategic tool, it can provide the missing link to help deliver better outcomes for citizens in a more sustainable way. This is not to dispute the school of thought that sees these initiatives as nothing but optimistic endeavors with unavoidable 'digital disconnect', which refers to the gap between the potential of digital transformation and the poor track record of the public sector to implement anything—a valid assertion that I suppose cannot be avoided, especially with a government that has proven beyond reasonable doubt that it is incapable of doing anything right, even the bare minimum. But, nonetheless, we can't just fold our arms and do nothing. Something has to give, or someone needs to say something, like I am trying to do with this book.

One is not naïve to the fact that this is indeed a complex endeavor with its own risks. Hence, I can imagine some wondering what I have been smoking to even imagine such a crazy idea in a country where corruption, looting, and dysfunction is so normalised. All I am saying is that citizens need to be angry enough to try, and they must cut out this evil 'boogeyman' of a government along with all the existing political parties which I believe are the true cancer and root cause of all the problems the public has. Achieving such a crazy level of reform in a country with two opposing extremes of the economic spectrum will require everyone to coordinate their efforts to develop the right policies, regulations, and infrastructure to enable a thriving digital economy that is free from the political charlatans and commercial hyenas. An 'all-hands-on-deck' collaboration between government departments, agencies, businesses, entrepreneurs, universities, NGOs, and citizens themselves that are willing to pull their knowledge and resources together in order to produce better outcomes for all is a given and a no-brainer.

In their article, Bertrand and McQueen suggest that the following steps are necessary in the development of this digital form of government:

• Create a conducive environment for the development of an inclusive digital economy.

• Engage and incentivise private businesses to help deliver the necessary infrastructure, train a digitally literate workforce, and enable secure access to services.

• Develop and invest in high-speed, reliable, and robust digital infrastructure, such as advanced telecom networks that include 5G networks and data centres.

• Establish state-of-the-art infrastructure that effectively addresses urban-rural and economic divides and promotes digital inclusion across the board.

• Introduce digital user identity and authentication that will enable citizens to gain seamless access to services.

• Formulate a national digital strategy that explicitly details the plans to deliver efficient and accessible public services while optimising the citizen experience and cutting out the corrupt 'middleman' (i.e., the government and political parties)—such strategy should ensure that all stakeholders involved are focused on nationwide outcomes and that funding is in place for cross-agency programs.

• Continually update regulatory and legal frameworks to take account of rapidly evolving technologies such as artificial intelligence (AI)—these frameworks should allow innovation to flourish while managing potential risks.

• Deal effectively with the threat of cyber-attacks using blockchain technology in order to avoid threats on the democratic process itself—this will involve embedding cybersecurity at every stage of the activities, from strategy to design and operations, and creating a robust cybersecurity policy framework and secure ecosystem for our imagined digital state.

• Compete with the private sector to recruit, train, and retain the best talent.

• Prepare the workforce for the digital age by building core technical skills such as software development and systems architecture, as well as new skills such as data science.

• Build a more dynamic environment that attracts younger workers in search of roles where they can make a difference to society and their lives.

• Consider the impact of automation on society, equality, and employment by developing the skills of the wider population to grow and maintain employment opportunities.

• Develop a clear vision of desired outcomes for the country around which all citizens can align, and then assess the role that digital technologies will play.

• Develop a digital strategy and implementation plan that translates the country's vision into reality.

• Reshape all state-owned entities and government departments, roles, and skills to provide a citizen-centric approach.

• Use design thinking and customer experience labs, rather than traditional government structures, to help build services around real user needs.

- Identify every technology, process, capability, and transition needed to digitise the entire citizen journey and make each touchpoint better, faster, and more efficient.
- Ensure that decision-making is transparent, and encourage the public's active involvement in planning, designing solutions, and guiding implementation.
- Create a more flexible IT infrastructure based on a service-oriented architecture, incorporating both traditional and contemporary models of infrastructure delivery to facilitate interoperability and information sharing.
- Integrate disparate legacy systems to provide a single view of the citizen.
- Use automation technologies, such as software robotics, as a cost-effective bridge between big IT implementations and manual processes.
- Build capabilities in areas such as emerging technologies, digital marketing, user-centred design, data analytics, and information security.
- Provide well-defined career paths—digital specialists may be a new breed of talent for the country.
- Encourage an innovation-oriented and entrepreneurial culture and empower the public at all levels to challenge the status quo for a better future independent of political hyenas (i.e., cut out the 'middleman').
- Use incentives like reward and recognition programs, if need be, in order to instil a focus on better outcomes for citizens.
- Set realistic milestones and timelines for the transformation program and develop tangible performance measures to demonstrate both short- and long-term results.
- Gather performance data on a regular basis to provide insights that can influence further planning and decision-making.

• Monitor citizen perceptions and satisfaction by investing in experience-measurement tools—these types of tools will also, in time, help to rebuild public trust.

In an age of digital disruption, governments can no longer act in isolation. Instead, they must tap into the knowledge and resources of the wider ecosystem—including start-ups, small and medium-sized enterprises (SMEs), entrepreneurs, universities and research institutions, civil society, and citizens themselves—to find innovative solutions to public policy challenges.

Governments across the globe are increasingly looking to harness emerging and disruptive technology solutions to improve the efficiency and effectiveness of public services, but remember, this is referring to governments that actually *want* to improve their public services; in other words, not the ones we find all over the African continent. The fast-growing "GovTech" market provides opportunities for new, creative digital solutions across the entire public sector value chain, from policymaking through to service delivery. Government agencies are also partnering or contracting with third parties to harness new technology-enabled business models that provide both the innovation required to transform existing services and the cost savings to make it viable.

Digital marketplaces are being created, and new procurement practices are being adopted which offer several benefits. These new mechanisms diversify the digital supplier base by reducing reliance on larger contractors, enabling governments to negotiate better contract terms and improve value for money, and fostering innovative solutions from non-traditional suppliers such as SMEs and start-ups.

Governments and public authorities across the world are launching open-data initiatives and setting up data-exchange platforms. The focus is on making data widely available to third parties, including citizens, to help develop new solutions to complex problems and to become more transparent and accountable. This is also helping to improve service delivery across a wide range of areas, such as education, health, environment, social protection, and finance. Citizens have a major role to play as a source of fresh ideas to help build a more efficient and effective public sector. Many governments have created digital platforms for public consultation on government policies and budget priorities—as seen in countries like Canada, Denmark, New Zealand, and Portugal, just to name a few—giving citizens more of a say in the day-to-day decisions that affect their lives, and the most innovative governments actively engage citizens in the ongoing co-production of policies and services. Policy labs are springing up everywhere to capture citizens' contributions to policymaking in areas as diverse as education, health, and justice.

However, as imaginative as the idea is that I have outlined above, I can assure you that no African country will buy into it, let alone entertain it and at least try to poke holes in it to test its viability or potential. The primary reason being that any state of disaster will always be a state of prosperity for others. No corrupt official that is benefitting from the current status quo would advocate for a more transparent system that is free of human exploitation and manipulation. The disparity between the rich and poor is what makes economies flourish. The invisible hand of the market system fails when everyone is rich or everyone is poor. The world is designed in a manner where there should always be a coexistence of light and darkness, wealth and poverty, academics and illiterates, evils and saints, black and white, slaves and masters, etc., while everyone is fighting for the middle ground just to keep their heads above water.

Despite all that is said and done and me rambling about cutting out the 'middleman' and shifting power to the people, one might argue that swapping out the 'middleman' from a government to technology, record labels to distribution channels, publisher to self-publishing, broadcaster to production houses, is not actually cutting out the 'middleman', but rather shifting from one 'middleman' to another, except the new 'middleman' may offer a better deal with less exploitation.

Indeed, the internet is meant to put the 'middleman' out of business and link buyers and sellers directly. However, I will be the first one to admit that it hasn't worked out that way thus far. From music trading networks to VOD platforms, the web has created new, uniquely potent intermediaries. Consumers can now negotiate better deals directly with the producers or sellers of the products thanks to technology and automated services in the market. This is a new form of 'middleman' or cyberspace that seeks to portray itself as a mere conduit, bearing little or no responsibility for what others do with its services and transactions. Some creatives argue that the legal ramifications remain hazy with this new 'middleman' and pose moral questions on what society should expect from this less evil 'boogeyman'. Artists are demanding the 'middleman' to take some responsibility for enabling an environment where widespread copying of music has become prevalent and effectively helping thousands of web users to steal creatives' intellectual property. Whereas the new 'middleman' maintains that they are nothing but simply the guy in the middle.

Nevertheless, throughout history, the 'middleman' has always been known as the parasite, exploiter, and profiteer who adds nothing of value to a product or service and yet unnecessarily increases the cost of goods and services being sold. Hence, the idea is that without going through a 'middleman' of any kind, the goods and services consumers purchase will always be cheaper but of the same quality as if purchased directly from the source. Everyone hates the markup. I mean, I understand the logic behind the convenience and efficiency that comes with some 'middleman' enterprises, but my problem is when governments are trying to do the same and still do a terrible job at it or don't even deliver the services people paid for through their taxes. Additionally, problems arise when the 'middleman' strikes a deal with the producer for exclusivity of supply so that none of the consumers who choose to do so can purchase directly from the producer. That is when the system gets flawed and corrupted for me. It is similar to politics, where political parties pull all the stops to stall the idea of independents running for office in provincial and national elections, which is a right that every adult citizen has (in terms of the Constitution) to stand as an independent candidate to be elected to municipalities, provincial legislatures, or the National Assembly, despite the resistance of the political hyenas that are still gung-ho on political party representation.

I am probably one of the few creatives in the African continent that advocates for an e-government or e-democracy. I strongly believe that South Africa is too far gone down the rabbit hole to strengthen democracy and transparency and eradicate corruption in the traditional way. Nothing can ever transform our country or renew its conscience, except for eliminating politicians or political parties altogether in the affairs of running and managing the country, especially if the intention is still to empower all citizens and facilitate citizen engagement. In my view, e-democracy is by far the only alternative left to foster participation and promote social inclusion.

PUBLIC BROADCASTING ENTERPRISES

The broadcast industry has also had its own fair share of digital revolutions which have completely disrupted its market across the globe. Television is the prime example, with digitalisation that has transformed the production, distribution, and consumption patterns of video content and reshaped the competitive environment of traditional broadcast enterprises. Rapid technological changes have created a wave of new opportunities—attracting competitors beyond the linear broadcast industries to challenge the long-standing incumbents—and an explosion of digital choices has excited, confused, and overwhelmed consumers who have responded by significantly altering their audio-visual consumption habits and expectations. Netflix is a perfect case study of an entity that walked away from the abuse of the existing establishments of the time and carved out its own path, regardless of the criticism and ridicule it experienced at the time of its inception. It started out as a traditional pay -per-view DVD rental service via mail, and then, in 1999, it decided to pivot into a subscription model wherein customers would pay a monthly fee for unlimited DVD rentals (and eventually the online streaming service we know today). This was an unprecedented, game-changing move that earned Netflix a great deal of criticism and scepticism at the time, but it was a move that allowed them to take over the market and put traditional movie rental companies like Blockbuster out of business. This trajectory is attributed to the growth of the internet and digitisation, and a phenomenon where advancing digital infrastructure has attracted new competition with different resources and motivations.

Companies that used to focus their operations on production, distribution, technical transmission, and device manufacturing are now exploring opportunities to integrate both vertically and horizontally. All of a sudden, traditional linear broadcasting companies are competing with large, multinational conglomerates that have access to global audiences and have now expanded their search for content to fill up their inventory—a market demand that has altered and given birth to new, flexible acquisition models while fees continue to rise. This shift in the media business landscape required traditional linear broadcasters to think differently about how they develop digital strategies that leverage existing resources while also extending their offering into alternative digital spaces in order to make up for the diminishing traditional audiences. This shift also requires a different type of evolutionary fitness, with appreciation of the fact that the days are gone where traditional linear and public broadcast enterprises enjoyed uncontested monopolies that thrived as a result of the state's protection and/or the lack of competition and alternative offerings from the market. I argue that adequate strategy responses to fundamental market shifts like these are warranted in order to avoid the possibility of becoming obsolete, much like public broadcasting services have become over the years across the globe.

The first technological discontinuity saw Pay TV networks (like DSTV) grow exponentially, and then recently the discontinuity of VOD/OTT disruption saw a plethora of multiple specialised platforms taking over and providing consumers convenience, speed, and affordability to consume premium content wherever and whenever they want to. However, this VOD/OTT frenzy has also come with its own fair share of criticism. Scholars are arguing that it too has reached its state of maturity, and big tech companies are already thinking about and exploring their next strategic moves to seize new markets and build new capabilities in order to remain competitive following the streaming maturity season. Whereas, in stark contrast, the public broadcasting enterprises are still twiddling their thumbs and begging for bailouts from the state with no innovative solutions and strategic plans to conquer or dominate the market in the interest of the public.

The fact that public broadcasting enterprises in Africa have missed out on both technological discontinuities (broadcast network technology and OTT streaming technology) and played the victim of both technological disruptions is a calamity and a display of despicable mediocrity. If public broadcasting enterprises such as the British Broadcasting Corporation (BBC) and Aljazeera are able to adapt to these rapidly changing market conditions and deliver both the public service mandate and the commercial interests of the institutions while still serving both the public and the shareholders involved, what is preventing the African public broadcasting enterprises from doing the same, other than concluding that they are rife with incompetence and corruption?

Despite my assertions about how incompetent and useless public broadcasting enterprises have become over the years, and advocating for cutting out the 'middleman' and allowing markets to compete freely and fairly (thereby giving the consumer all the power to choose freely who they want to do business with/consume products from without being abused and exploited by a corrupt system that adds no value except to collude and fix prices at their expense), public broadcasting enterprises remain the only type of 'middleman' I wish could be preserved and strengthened. This is purely based on their noble founding principles and intentions that have, over the years, suffered manipulation by corrupt officials both commercially and politically to serve the interests of individuals who could care less about the wellbeing of the public, let alone the sustainability of these entities.

Just because a concept has been badly executed and abused over the years by the 'boogeyman' to a state of collapse, it doesn't mean that it's a bad concept to begin with. I'm not going to spend time defending the importance of the public broadcasting service and the key role that it plays in democratic society in the sense that it preserves the function of democracy by holding both the public and private elite accountable. My intention is to argue that public broadcasting enterprises are the type of 'boogeyman' I label as 'the middleman with a heart'. You know, that type of drug lord or mafia boss that makes sure no one robs or sells drugs in the neighbourhood where he resides. I am referring to the type of 'gangster' that stands up for the weak and vulnerable (especially when private media is now associated with bullying, fake news, underhanded business practices, and doing anything and everything to gain audiences and profit margins regardless of the societal impact of what they broadcast or report on) and, furthermore, protects and pushes the veiled Eurocentric agendas and propaganda of those that own and control the means of production in the interest of capturing the state or influencing economic policy directions to further their own economic interests.

Public broadcasting enterprises are not difficult ones to lead and transform by removing politicians, corrupt employees, and greedy, incompetent suppliers. There is nothing that strategic management theories and concepts cannot solve, as long as everything is done with genuine intentions of servicing the public and delivering the same constitutional mandates the enterprise is regulated and obligated to deliver, including revenue generation which is a task that many formally trained strategic managers and orthodox-trained media practitioners should understand. This requires executive leaders that embody all-in-one academic, commercial, creative, innovative, and strategic skills—with public broadcasting service credentials—to grasp all the technical and nuanced debates about reconciling the opposing interests of growing audiences and generating revenue while also keeping all stakeholders involved satisfied. Leaders that are able to synergistically transform these enterprises by exploiting existing resources and integrating new ones while improving operating efficiencies and deriving value from harmonising multichannel offerings.

This is a different type of ambidexterity where one doesn't only *understand* the paradox and tug of war between the public broadcasting system and commercial broadcasting viability of the enterprise, but is also able to *orchestrate* its resource base while sensing, seizing, or exploiting existing resources, exploring and integrating future opportunities, and neutralising threats faced by the enterprises. In my view, central to the public broadcasting enterprise's problems is its inability to derive value from existing commercial assets, instead continuing with this opaque business model where public service assets are the ones generating higher audience ratings and revenue with profit margins that supersede those of the commercial assets they own.

Here we have a broken strategic system, or a complete lack thereof, where public assets are now forced to subsidise the so-called 'commercial brands' of the public broadcast enterprise, perhaps suggesting that either something is wrong with the product offered to consumers by public broadcasters, the brand positioning and alignment of the public broadcasting assets is not adequately researched, the customer targeted by public broadcasting enterprises is misdiagnosed and mis-targeted, there is no strategy altogether, or there are zero competences in terms of skills and expertise to master ordinary capabilities, let alone develop and build new dynamic capabilities required to reverse the status quo.

Grouping strategic resources into market-oriented and internal resources reinforces the necessary shift towards customer-centric business strategies. My assertion is that public broadcasting enterprises claim to be operating in the interest of the public, yet the very same public is leaving them for alternative offerings from new and more competitive players at a price higher than what public broadcasting enterprises charge—a phenomenon which suggests that perhaps the so-called 'public interest' that public broadcasting enterprises claim to be delivering is actually not the interest of the public, if that same public is running away from it.

Hence, the fundamental question becomes, whose interest is then being served by the public broadcasting enterprises if not the public's? This is a genuine question that is not aimed at accusing public broadcasting enter-prises of serving external interests or its own evolutionary fitness. Rather, it is a conundrum that makes it difficult to argue against proponents of free markets and the dissolu-tion of public broadcasting enterprises both as an outdated concept that media markets no longer need, and as mouth pieces for private sector propaganda and anti-public political agendas used to manipulate the poor to keep voting and putting the evil 'middleman' into power while purchasing the same unhealthy products that sustain the indignity and poverty of the marginalised masses. However, being an optimist and a proponent of the plurality of views and the understanding of how the poor can benefit from accessing information and education through public media enterprises, I believe that public and private media can indeed coexist while both commercial and social interests are delivered for everyone to win.

I can't help but believe that, as exciting and disruptive as the aforementioned technological discontinuities have been, it is a devastating sight to witness traditional media and public broadcasting enterprises struggle to keep up with the changing market conditions. Public broadcasting service enterprises are the weakest 'middlemen', feeling most of the brunt due to a myriad of reasons that can be attributed to all of its stakeholders involved both internally and externally. It is undeniable that public broadcasting enterprises have been suffering at the hands of external forces who are determined to capture their audiences and the advertising slice of the pie. However, there is also something to be said about the internal strategic blunders that have crippled these institutions for a number of years now.

I classify these blunders as organisational 'own goals', including insufficient financial resources, inexperienced leadership in broadcasting, mismanagement of resources, skills shortage, corruption, changing market conditions, inadaptability, weak strategic thinking, heavy reliance on regulatory remits, and ill-informed strategic management decisions (or lack thereof). This is an assertion that, for obvious reasons, no one would like to admit or take accountability for, instead being more likely to level the challenges squarely on the predecessors who created the mess in the first place or couldn't predict the future market conditions.

This short-sighted, selective prism of analysis was designed by the public broadcaster to absolve themselves of all the failures to turn things around despite the so-called 'radical decisions' that were made to make the organisation lean, mean, and fit for purpose. What is this purpose, though, if the revenue generation of public broadcasting enterprises has regressed, the market share eroded, audiences declined, and organisational culture diminished? However, despite all this, the power of public broadcasting enterprises as the 'middlemen' is undeniable, even in an environment where technology has empowered people to move from what traditional linear broadcasters would pre-schedule for appointment viewing to watching pre-selected content anytime, anywhere, and on a device of their choice.

The discussion will always come back with issues unrelated to business or market conditions and ones more focused on greed, corruption, complaisance, and unqualified power that is aimed at looting and exploiting both the supplier and consumer. In this case, both the production house companies and the viewers are bearing the brunt of the epic failures of public broadcasting enterprises, while the private media cares about nothing else except for profit levels and social media trends (if shows like *Cheaters*, *The Real Housewives* of whatever city, *Uyajola 9/9*, and many more are anything to go by). This is a painful part of the discussion where I dare say that the public broadcasting 'middleman' ought not to be cut completely, but instead *assisted* in transforming itself into a different type of 'middleman' that can be managed better and equipped with more skilled and qualified personnel that understand the paradox of public broad-casting systems in the era of rapid technological change.

Furthermore, these enterprises should employ capable men and women who understand that public broadcasting enterprises are deliberately destroyed by all stakeholders, including the creative arts industry, government, citizens, production houses, suppliers, employees, the regulator, and the competition. Everyone is looking out for themselves and their own bottom line, regardless of how the public gets affected. If corruption was not the name of the game and the driving force behind the media and creative arts industry, it would be worth noting that a successful public broadcasting service, as an ideology, is a good idea for the prosperity of creative arts and electronic media industries; whereas the death of it is nothing but an absolute catastrophe for the media landscape at large.

Hence, transforming public broadcasting services and restoring their dignity and public trust can only happen when those that run them begin to take these enterprises seriously, starting with their organisational strategic visions and missions. Most of these institutions tend to have very ambiguous visions and missions that do not inspire confidence and are so detached and misaligned from what the institutions are and what they want to be, let alone where they want to go. What does it mean when one of the public enterprises says their vision is to be "the face of Africa"? How does that give them any competitive advantage amid the shifting market conditions? How does that relate to the enterprise's dynamic capabilities? How does the staff operationalise that with their daily activities and deliverables? How do they reconcile their competing public service mandate and commercial enterprise deliverables with that type of vision? How is that vision unique to them as a brand? Business scholars will tell you that the vision of an ambitious enterprise has to be "SMART"—Specific, Measurable, Attainable, Realisable, and Timely—and anything other than these guidelines will get the enterprise nowhere.

Research shows that in 2024, the real currency of our age is data, attention, and time, especially when the internet and other forms of technology are rearranging the world with alarming frequency. Hence, creative and innovative thinkers who produce products and services drive these economies, including content creators. It is no surprise that public broadcasting enterprises are no longer the first point of call for producers when they have concepts or ideas, as these tasks demand a caliber of leaders that can envision future possibilities of the concepts and be able to enlist others to share in such a vision. A caliber of leaders which the public broadcasters simply do not have. Regardless of the type of organisation or sector one leads, no one can strive for excellence and mastery without a vision. Hence, people without a unifying vision to facilitate their collaborations and achieve outcomes and outputs will always struggle. A "SMART" vision provides a clear mental image of what one wishes to achieve and in which direction the organisation should be steered, thereby articulating the organisation's primary goals and ambitions. Without a clear future, there is no way to prioritise decisions and shape the organisation's strategy. Therefore, it is highly unlikely for the organisation to grow, as there is no clear indication of its direction for growth and improvement.

A vision cannot just be an academic exercise or a vague idea to tick a box and sound like you have something worthwhile on your hands. A vision needs to be exciting and needs to energise everyone working towards achieving it. It needs to be believable, relevant, realistic, bring about credibility, provide a sense of purpose, and be inspirational; otherwise, the organisation fails. An attractive vision creates a future that people want to be part of and that individuals are motivated to work towards. It includes a guiding philosophy of principles and values that stem from the organisation's core beliefs and purpose. It creates meaning in the organisation and is the main tool that leaders use to guide it. It enables leaders to inspire, attract, and energise their followers.

A vision is the energy of the organisation, as it provides something for the members of that organisation to believe in and creates a common ownership. It is for that reason that I argue perhaps the root cause of most public broadcasting enterprises' problems, and why they struggle to respond to new market changes, is their weak visions that appear ambiguous and vague, don't serve as motivators to create enthusiasm about the organisation's future and increase employee commitment, and don't create a sense of belonging and meaning to establish a connection between employees and the organisation, which would help them find meaning in their work.

A vision should provide a link between the present and the future, with particular focus on the future, to ensure clarity on the organisation's direction. A shared sense of purpose helps employees understand what they are working towards and how their efforts contribute to the organisation. It is a phenomenon that spills over from the quality of the internal output to the external operations of content delivery by production houses and the quality of their concepts and production value—a win-win scenario that culminates in benefits for the creative arts industry, the artists, and the public.

Like many other organisations, including private sector businesses, creative organisations are political arenas in which different stakeholders have competing interests and influence decision-making. Hence, it is not a surprise to see public broadcasting enterprises across the globe drifting away from being constitutionally enshrined broadcasters that are meant to be creative, innovative, and editorially astute entities that educate, inform, and entertain while delivering their commercial sustainability and unfunded mandates, and instead rapidly turning into more failed SOEs that are a burden to the public purse and follow in the footsteps of other public institutions that have failed to innovate in the advent of big technological discontinuities.

Public broadcasters are too inward-looking, metaphorically driving a car on full throttle with the handbrake up. They find themselves in a self-inflicted conundrum, with the majority of their personnel drunk on their own hype and believing that they are still a force to be reckoned with, whereas the ship has long sailed and is still stuck at the shoreline of distress. This phenomenon has, in recent years, culminated into production houses being treated disrespectfully by junior staff members of the broadcasters who have never produced a thing in their lives. A ripple effect permeating the industry and leaving broadcasters with no credible suppliers but rather corrupt, inexperienced, and desperate production companies that will do anything and everything to grease the hand that feeds them.

At the same time, some seasoned, experienced, and skilled suppliers are getting headhunted and invited to closed pitches by international broadcasters (that I allege to be complicit in the demise of public broadcasting enterprises), while others resort to strictly doing commercials and advertiser-funded programming (AFP) to keep their businesses afloat and avoid the stress of dealing with public broadcasting service bureaucracy that serves no one but aligned and closely-connected cronies.

Another thing that happens in the public broadcasting environment, similarly to any state-owned entity, are untenable levels of decision-making biases. An astonishing realisation is that, when it comes to the content we see on TV, there is no scientific matrix used to decide what would make the content successful after selecting it for commission or license. Instead, it is all based on gut feeling, intuition, or a thumb-suck that hinges on the historic performance of the slot, genre, and experience of the producer in creating similar work, compounded with marketing investment and simply 'hoping for the best'. This is unlike digital platforms, where analytics are extremely precise and detailed and can project performances with utmost accuracy and probability of success, thereby impacting decision-making for future acquisitions.

This unscientific level of bias distorts the way that information is acquired, interpreted, and used in decision-making processes. It is something that I believe public broadcasting enterprise leaders are vulnerable to and includes decision traps, such as the following:

1. Positive bias: Individuals avoid or dismiss information that threatens their positive motivation. Public broadcasting leaders suffer a lot from this form of bias, and they always seek employees that validate whatever they say.

2. Control illusion: The illusion that people have more control over the effect of their actions than they actually do. This is a type of bias that is also prevalent in public institutions and often equates to the 'Dunning Kruger Effect' (i.e., a phenomenon in which people with limited competence in their given domains overestimate their abilities) that most bullies within these public broadcasting enterprises suffer from.

3. Escalating commitment: A positive bias and control illusion resulting in the reluctance to abandon a course of action that has failed to yield dividends, based on the presumed soundness of the reasoning that led to the decision. A typical example of this bias would be the obsession with digital terrestrial television (DTT) thirty years later despite it failing to be switched on by the public broadcaster's shareholders who were too busy debating whether or not to encrypt, and questions meandering around the industry circles about who would get the tender to manufacture and distribute the set top boxes. Whereas, in the meantime, the entire world has moved on to OTT platforms and streaming services for cheaper rates, faster technologies, and larger audiences.

4. Confirmation bias: Decisions are based on inadequate or incomplete information and seek to confirm a preferred hypothesis, and any information that negates that hypothesis gets ignored. This is a form of bias common in the public broadcaster's boardrooms where ideas are not necessarily pressure tested. Things often come as instructions with no intellectual engagement among colleagues who seek to win each other over on facts. Instead, those who possess some power by the offices they occupy, or by shouting the loudest, come with pre-determined outcomes and defend propositions with everything they have to purely seek validation.

5. Omission neglect: A common form of bias where missing information, absent knowledge, and acts of omission are not considered in making decisions.

6. Salience bias: More prominent information is emphasised, and less prominent information is ignored. (Remember the '80/20' and '90/10' decisions made by the public broadcaster for content acquisitions in television and radio respectively?)

7. Action bias: Seen as more advantageous than not acting, optimism is valued and pessimism is equated to disloyalty. Time constraints compel decision makers to justify why they are not acting even though it's a valid option to do so.

8. Anchoring: Initial estimates or judgements sway decision makers towards emotionally preferred decisions, preventing them from adjusting their choice based on new or disconfirming opinions.

9. Effect heuristic: For preferred options where risks are minimised and potential benefits are exaggerated. I always questioned this whenever I looked at the sales projections within the public broadcasting enterprise, wondering about the accuracy of the matrix used to determine each of the preferred ROI of what is to be acquired.

These biases can manifest in business when a leader is driven by the desire to pursue disastrous projects while dismissing any warning signs, an unfortunate state of affairs that I believe is common and prevalent in most public broadcasting enterprises as they sing for their lunch and try to appease their veiled handlers. For this 'middleman' to survive, a lot needs to change. We cannot, year in and year out, debate the validity of these enterprises' existence and why the public should continue to pay for their mismanagement. Einstein once said, "insanity is doing the same thing over and over and expecting different results." How many times have you heard elders talk about history being the best teacher when carving a pathway for the future? Yet, for as long as I can remember, the public stood witness to several reports from different stakeholders—including those who are supposed to be siding with the public broadcaster— peddling what some scholars call logical fallacies.

Logical fallacies are what we sometimes confuse with cognitive bias, which is not the same concept. Rather, logical fallacies are flaws in seemingly logical arguments that undermine soundness and credibility and lead decision makers to erroneous conclusions. Logical fallacies include the following:

1. Sunk cost fallacy: A behavior or endeavor that is continued based on the previous investment of resources, including time, money, or effort. (For example, take a look at the South African public broadcaster commissioning the same soapie on primetime for over thirty years, spending more than R100 million per season for just half the audiences the show once had.)

2. Planning fallacy: Decision makers that focus exclusively on the present cases or projects.

3. Gamble's fallacy: Random events are linked and assumed to become less random and more predictable when repeated.

The public broadcasting enterprise's inability to amount to anything of commercial significance and legitimacy is exactly the culmination of the aforementioned fallacies, which I believed always informed the decision making in these institutions as opposed to proper scientific research. If the public broadcasting enterprises are genuine about turning themselves around, research must become part of what informs every sphere of their operations. This is not to say that research is the magic wand, or a 'be all and end all' solution to 'un-screwing' the enterprises; it is merely highlighting that making the right decisions will come with the territory, especially in a pressurised and rapidly changing environment such as the one found in media industries across the globe. It is crucial for leaders to obtain relevant information and compare alternatives before choosing a course of action.

Although quantitative data appears to be more reliable than this more qualitative data, it might be just what the public broadcasting enterprises need, as most of their problems and challenges appear nuanced and qualitative in nature.

In 2018, Chris Kurtarna, a top executive leadership scholar and Doctor in Politics from the University of Oxford, proposed four sins of certainty, and I believe that the public broadcaster of South Africa suffers from two of them. The first two sins are named hubris and myopia. Hubris refers to high levels of arrogance, while myopia refers to the short-sightedness that results from overconfidence on the part of the leaders running the organisation. (The last two sins of certainty are paralysis and angst, which I will not be focusing on.) Leaders can counteract hubris by managing and planning for risks, and they can counteract myopia by challenging information and encouraging discussion and debate, something that seems to be foreign to the public broadcasting enterprises if their success rate (or lack of success) is anything to go by.

Quite often in the creative arts industry and the broadcasting network sector, the pace of change becomes increasingly faster, a truism we repeatedly hear in all corners of the media industry. Professor Micheal Smets, who, like Kurtarna, is also a scholar of executive leadership, talks about the S-Cube model of change, arguing that the world has always been changing faster than ever before (if one tracks as far back as the nineties, eighties, seventies, etc.), and people have always felt this; therefore, perhaps the speed at which the world is changing is not a dimension within which the public broadcasting enterprises should think when change is concerned.

Like Professor Smets suggests, rather than thinking about the *speed* of change that the public broadcasting enterprises are struggling to keep up with, perhaps we should think about the *scope* and *significance* of that change. Speed is about evolutionary trends we can see coming, and for which we can adjust, pivot, and brace for impact. Whereas there are revolutionary things that take everyone by surprise, are disruptive, and are changing faster than ever. Although the world is indeed changing faster than before, it doesn't mean that our world *and* the public broadcaster's world is changing faster than ever before, or that all parts of the world are changing at the same pace.

What I am trying to say is that the *scope* within which things are changing is perhaps what the public broadcaster needs to focus on instead of the speed, especially judging by the myriad of challenges the organisation is faced with—both known and unknown, or visible and invisible. Professor Smets talks a lot about scope and significance, asserting that when it comes to the 'scope' of change, we must not worry much about how fast problems are coming our way but rather how big they are, and my advice to the public broadcaster is that, now more than ever before, it needs to pay attention to the *scope* of change, as it has a domino effect on the entire public and the creative arts industry, including those still in higher learning institutions and wishing to enter this industry. This focuses on a distinction between how the trends affect a single unit versus those that are systemic.

When it comes to 'significance' of change, it's not just about how fast the trends are approaching, but how big the challenges are and how profound their impact is. A good question to ask is whether we can respond to this trend through a technical change, operational twig, or tactical adjustment, or if we must fundamentally rebuild the entire organisation from scratch, which is what

Professor Tim Morris, a director of the Executive Leadership Program at the Saïd Business School at Oxford University calls "foundational challenges". These are the insights found and acquired by taking some time and investing in acquiring knowledge in order to think of potential solutions strategically and not just 'wing it' based on political connections, bullying, or shouting the loudest, as we've seen over the years in public broadcasting institutions.

For the public broadcaster to be 'un-screwed', and to help 'un-screw' the entire creative arts industry in the process, the current and next leadership must begin to think differently and trust the human capital within the organisation to steer the ship in the right direction. The continuum of knowing is made up of data, analysis, intellect, and cognitive capabilities. It's not rocket science; all that is required is ethical leadership that is honest, loving, caring, empathetic, and empowering.

In this sense, power refers to the ability to gain people's co-operation to carry out plans, projects, or tasks, not the toxic power of intimidation and victimisation that we've witnessed over the years in the public broadcasting institutions. Tim Morris asserts that, "While an individual can be powerful and influence others without occupying a leadership position, a person cannot be a leader without acquiring power and exercise influence". Leaders use their power to transform their vision for the future into reality. This includes different forms of power, such as legitimate power, expertise power, and referent power. At an organisational level, power often resides in departments and business units that either control valuable resources or can solve critical problems/are perceived to be the ones that can solve critical problems for the organisation. For a supposedly creative institution such as the public broadcasting enterprise, creativity can never be relegated to the periphery of the business, especially when it comes to the development of the turnaround strategy. Central to the public broadcasting enterprise's demise is the lack of appreciation for the role creativity has played over the years in sustaining their business and maintaining their market dominance.

Creativity is not just an aesthetic concept designed for the sake of being 'cool' or appearing to be 'down' with the latest trends. Rather, it is one of the most important disciplines that challenges conventional wisdom and breaks patterns and habits to gain advantages. Apart from the plethora of organisations that have already benefitted from harvesting their creative strategies across different sectors around the globe, creativity continues to prove itself as a powerful tool with revolutionary effects that can turn around any institution, generating greater job or employee satisfaction while also delivering positive and commercially sound results for shareholders. However, the fact of the matter is that, over the years, public broadcasting enterprises have relegated creativity to the periphery of their business and operations, and this is evident in the manner in which the board and the executive management team have been appointed. Sidelining creative broadcasters away from running and managing creative businesses (such as public broadcasting enterprises) is the most redundant practice I have ever seen in the history of the broadcast business, and it is a phenomenon that explains why these institutions have, over the years, ceased to be creative and have transformed into the lethargic, bureaucratic, unimaginative institutions that fail more than they succeed.

You will never find any creative professional or media practitioner appointed to lead financial institutions, legal institutions, technology and engineering institutions, medical institutions, logistics companies, etc. Yet, year in and year out, creative businesses—including public broadcasters—are continuously hiring candidates that are either accountants, lawyers, theologians, teachers, or grade eleven dropouts, and they still get shocked when all of them fail and end up bringing these institutions to bankruptcy and a state of collapse. Hence, I continue to allege that the failure of public broadcasting enterprises is not by mistake; it's a deliberate, man-made disaster aimed at destroying the public broadcasting enterprise in order to make way for private media enterprises to consolidate the market and sustain a continental monopoly. A successful public broadcasting enterprise can never be a great thing for private media enterprises; therefore, it is in private media's best interest to ensure the public broadcaster's demise, even if it means paying their way through employees, suppliers, politicians, the board, or the regulator for that matter.

This is a conspiracy which I assert can be achieved through secret partnerships between all stakeholders involved, including employees, management, the board, the shareholders, the regulator, the suppliers, media-monitoring NGOs, and many more. Contrary to the small-time, petty allegations of corruption and bribery between suppliers (i.e., production houses and marketing/event agencies) and public service officials, I believe that there is a bigger invisible hand, with deep pockets, that is orchestrating the rapid fall of the public broadcasting enterprise to ensure that no stone is left unturned in burying these institutions to a point where they can be sold for a miniscule amount, like we have seen happening with the national carrier. I mean, have you noticed lately how similar the private broadcast networks look to the public broadcaster? Exhibit A being the list of production house content suppliers they use, the on-air talent they use, the content they acquire, the prominence of vernacular languages on their channels, the adoption of *Nguni* news broadcasts, the marketing strategy targeting the lower Living Standards Measure (LSM) market, and the deliberate attempt to capture the masses through the monopolising of sports rights, particularly football. There is a bigger game plan at play, and I believe that every key strategic leader in the government is in on it.

Yes, things are no longer the same, as public broadcasting enterprises no longer hold the monopoly they once enjoyed. The market has grown significantly, with new competing entrants on the scene, including international streaming platforms, the reduction of data costs, and growing access to the internet, all compounded with the growing desire of everyone wanting to create their own content and distribute it through platforms such as YouTube, Instagram, X (formerly Twitter), Facebook, TikTok, etc. However, the most important thing I'm opining about is that public broadcasting enterprises need leaders that are both 'book' smart and 'street' smart, and possess incorruptible integrity and morals, in order to navigate the complexities of running a public broadcasting enterprise. It is not a difficult enterprise to turn around. When you truly understand broadcasting, it is by far the easiest institution to run, as long has you have the right men and women who are of ethical stature and who are nowhere near the political hyenas.

Sometimes the effectiveness of ethical leadership in South Africa is something that is taken for granted, yet this is an area of business the organisation's prosperity is dependent on in order to meet stakeholders' demands and needs (including the employees) and breed a culture of excellence. Hence, I argue that effective leadership at the public broadcaster is by far the one thing that can make a considerable difference in the endeavor to turn it around, especially given its complex nature in the midst of contemporary working environments. In order to end the public broadcasting corruption, mismanagement, and alleged political influence, these institutions desperately need *expert* power, not *political* power, which is a type of power that emanates from a leader's passion for specialist knowledge, skills, or abilities within a clearly defined functional area. To exercise this power, an individual must have the necessary credentials in broadcasting and creative industries, which most of the public broadcasting leaders in South Africa we've seen over the years seem to lack.

Specialist knowledge is becoming more and more important as organisations become increasingly complex and technologically advanced. Therefore, even individuals of a low rank in the organisational hierarchy who are acknowledged as experts in specified areas should be consulted by senior decision makers, a process which I opine is non-existent at the public broadcasting enterprise, as I believe they often value opinions that come from their political handlers more. This is a pandemic that then results in the screwing of the business and breeds a culture of silence and personnel doing the bare minimum to keep their jobs, watching things unfold while holding all the knowledge and solutions that could have assisted the organisation in the first place.

Regardless of how fast the world is changing and how fast new trends are infiltrating markets—including those in the broadcasting and creative arts sectors—one cannot afford to isolate institutional memory. Information and knowledge are forms of power that are not dissimilar to expert power and have considerable influence on individuals, teams, and other groups who possess information that others need to carry out their tasks effectively. The power of information is valuable in any context and can be strategically employed to achieve organisational goals.

Public broadcasting leaders who rely solely on the authority conferred upon them by their positions foster feelings of frustration, dissatisfaction, and resistance among their followers. What the leadership of public broadcasting enterprises possibly doesn't understand, and what I also think contributes to the fundamental erosion of these entities, is that personal power is a more vital determinant of employee satisfaction, performance, and commitment to organisational goals than positional power is. And, most importantly, it is an essential determinant of the perceived effectiveness of leaders and those who use their expert knowledge or charismatic personality to motivate and inspire their followers to create a climate of trust. In highly complex and collaborative organisations, formal authority is often insufficient on its own to secure the co-operation of a range of internal and external stakeholders. Thus, effective leaders increasingly rely on influence as a form of soft power that can persuade people to align with personal agendas and organisational goals.

Dare I say that perhaps creative arts professionals in the broadcasting and creative arts industry, as well as creative personnel working with/for the public broadcasting enterprises, have found themselves in the situations they are in due to their own inability to recognise and use their soft power of influencing change in the creative arts industry? Instead, they cry in dark corners and secluded corridors in fear of exclusion by the powerful owners of the production and distribution means. Power implies formal authority and control, while influence is more subtle and relies on persuasion to get people to buy into the vision. Now, if we call ourselves creatives, does it not beg the question of why we haven't utilised this form of creativity to turn the tide and transform our own creative arts industry? And public broadcasting enterprises, for that matter? The public service broadcasters desperately need to flatten their hierarchical structures to keep up with the latest creative business practices if they want to 'un-screw' themselves from the shackles of erosion and competitive disadvantage they find themselves in.

Influence allows leaders to guide the ideas and behavior of followers/individuals that they have no direct control or positional power over, including their peers and superiors. Something can be done using different strategies and tactics employed to influence others, such as pressure tactics, legitimising tactics, ingratiating tactics, exchange tactics, coalition tactics, consultation tactics, rational persuasion, upward appeals, and inspirational appeals—strategic tactics that I won't go into detail with but urge readers that are interested to read up on them.

It is no secret that the major problem faced by leaders within the public broadcasting enterprises, including creative artists, is the understanding of what we call the Model of Influence, which comprises four interrelated and essential steps that can help the public broadcasters to turn the tide around significantly:

• Establish credibility based on expertise and establish relationships with key individuals.

• Frame goals to emphasise mutual benefits and advantages to all parties and establish common ground with the audience.

• Reinforce the chosen position by presenting evidence that is compelling and combining quantitative data with anecdotes, examples, and metaphors.

• Connect emotionally with followers by demonstrating a personal commitment to their position and responding to their emotional state.

Now, with all the rambling and whining lectures I have given illustrating how we can strengthen public broadcasting enterprises instead of cutting them off (as I have been advocating for all the other 'middlemen' in previous chapters), it is quite obvious that I have a soft spot for the public broadcasting enterprises. However, this has nothing to do with me having worked for them for more than twenty-three years; rather, this comes from a deep-seated love I have for the founding principles on which the ideology behind the public broadcasting enterprises was conceptualised. I don't think the creative arts industry (specifically music, film, and television production house companies) comprehends the impact of not having public broadcasting services in our society. For those of you who are up-and-coming creative artists or creative content creators, in the absence of the internet, public broadcasting platforms are most likely the closest chance you might have for your work to access larger portions of your targeted audiences.

It is not a coincidence that for most of the so-called 'A-list' personalities you classify as celebrities, ninety-nine percent got their break from public broadcasting platforms. Privately owned media interests are all about the bottom line, and they are always looking for opportunities to leverage on in order to further their growth and competitiveness motivated by profit maximisation. Similar to aspiring content suppliers, you are most likely to get a commissioning and licensing deal with a public broadcasting enterprise, even despite all the corruption and political influence; whereas private media can afford to hide behind closed pitches and preferential procurement.

Likewise, for students that are still in arts and media schools, the probability of getting internship opportunities in the private media industry will diminish; whereas a public broadcasting environment can provide you with an opportunity to learn and grow while finding your niche. Private media doesn't have such obligations and doesn't owe anyone any explanation; they can run their business whichever way they like. Hence, the majority of music royalties and television repeat fees are most likely to be paid by the public broadcasting entities. Creating a route for public broadcasting enterprises to be the 'middleman' that is protected, preserved, and strengthened for the betterment of the creative arts industry and the public at large is the logical and right thing to do, especially in a country where levels of inequality are at an all-time high.

Access to education, information, and entertainment is becoming a basic need and a scarce commodity in this knowledge economy. Even more so with high unemployment rates where most citizens in far-flung, remote rural areas and townships cannot afford internet access or private media subscriptions. Therefore, in light of the recent discovery that the South African public broadcaster is on the brink of insolvency and might not even be able to meet its obligations, including paying salaries and suppliers, I'd like to propose four things the public broadcasting enterprise should work on with immediate effect, and these are Resource Orchestration, Dynamic Capabilities, Strategy Diversification, and Corporate Rebranding. However, to implement these four concepts, a strong level of ambidexterity is required while re-engineering a new vision that is 'SMART' and embodies all the ingredients of a good vision I outlined previously.

Essentially, being an ambidextrous organisation, which is what I'm calling for the public broadcaster to do, is in actual fact calling for management to plan a new path which will look backward and attend to the products and processes of the past while also gazing forward and preparing for innovations that will define the public broadcasting enterprise's future. The public broadcaster needs to employ a mental balancing act of exploring new opportunities while at the same time working diligently to exploit existing resources and capabilities, especially now that they are broke again and waiting with a begging bowl for yet another bailout from the public purse. Let's start with resource orchestration.

1. Resource Orchestration

• **Television** – In light of the fact that the public broadcasting enterprise doesn't have many platforms to bargain with for audiences and advertising revenue, my proposal is that perhaps the major orchestration of resources should start where the bulk of their costs come from and where the potential of making more money could emanate from (in this case, resources being the public broadcaster's programs, television channels, and radio stations).

Starting with the television channels, it is common knowledge that the public broadcasting enterprise of South Africa doesn't have many, an understanding that then suggests they can't afford to have long-running television shows that occupy the entire week of their schedule, especially with the soapie offering. Take, for example, the 6:30 pm, 8:00 pm and 8:30 pm slots. The public broadcaster has stripped these slots from Monday to Friday with shows that cost an average of R70 - R100 million per season—shows that have been on the schedule for almost ten years, with one of them nearing three decades of primetime screen time. This is an illogical business practice if you look at the audience ratings trajectory of these shows, where audiences are half of what they were ten years ago during the inception of these acquisitions. Not to mention the expenditure of these shows that have lost popularity and been rejected by audiences who are opting for better content coming from competing private media enterprises. Essentially what this means is that on one channel, the public broadcaster occupies fifteen primetime slots per week, with three underperforming soapies costing ten times the price they acquired them for.

I propose that this business reality and public broadcasting catastrophe be dealt with immediately by reducing all three of these soapies across the network into one day a week and 130 episodes per season. In addition, there should be a performance clause that demands an audience ratings performance review on episode twelve of the season, as well as intervention strategies to improve performance and serve as a warning of immediate termination on episode twenty-six if the show still fails to meet the audience targets. What this would then mean is that on one channel alone, you have opened up twelve more primetime slots for new long-running shows at half the commissioning price you are currently paying on failing properties, and you can replicate this across the entire television network, which means overnight you have twenty-eight more slots to fill with fresh, never-before-seen content to market to audiences, sell to advertisers, and commission to the production industry. That is twenty-eight more production houses that will gain work. Can you imagine how many jobs that is for the creative film and television industry?

Secondly, the public broadcaster needs to dismantle this so-called 'centralised' content hub/division and replace it with an innovative and creative hub while integrating all the editorial personnel into the new channels in order to speed up operational processes and tighten up accountability of content delivery and performance. Most of the challenges crippling the public broadcaster, particularly the television division, is this democratisation of decisions that results in inefficiencies, even in ordinary capabilities such as operations, administration, and governance. It makes no sense to have a business plan written and circulated to more than five officials before a decision is made, which explains why something as simple as drafting a standard contract will take six weeks to turn around. Commissioning editors will tell you that it'll take eighteen to twenty-four months to turn around a drama series, while the producers themselves are telling you a different story about how much more quickly they can turn that same series around. Automating all administrative processes for developing business plans, drafting contracts, content submissions, and approval systems is a bold decision that could yield immediate results which will not only increase the speed of doing business but also bring about new audiences, providing the sales team with enough to sell to advertisers while contributing to the development and growth of the film and television production industry and creating ever-needed jobs.

• **Henley** – The Henley facilities, located in the Henley Studio complex in Auckland Park, are by far the most underutilised resource the public broadcasting enterprise has. Henley is a technology and facility division where there are supposed to be production studios as well as offline and post-production facilities that can be used for both internal and external productions. However, these facilities have instead become dormant and redundant, with few internal on-air producers actually utilising them, a wasteful endeavor of the highest proportion.

They could generate unimaginable revenue if they are revamped and rebuilt into state-of-the-art facilities with the latest technologies and sufficient human capital to operate and manage them effectively. For example, the public broadcaster could develop a rate card for them that can be used to sell these facilities as rental spaces to the advertising industry, production industry, and to individuals seeking to create their own content.

One of the calamities resulting in the underutilisation of Henley facilities is the fact that the TV channels themselves commission shows that are produced in facilities owned by their competitors; whereas they have their own facilities that can do the job. How the public broadcaster can allow its key pillar properties to be produced and filmed in the premises of its competing broadcasters boggles my mind. What this means then is that the public broadcaster's competition can gain insight of the first offline drafts of the new shows even before the public broadcaster can see them. This is corporate naivety of highest degree. Spending money on your competitor to house and gain insight on new products you are building in order to compete with them, while still expecting to win the market share against them, is straight up foolish and has been happening (and will continue to happen) for years.

Part of this resource orchestration, perhaps after repurposing the Henley facilities, is to enforce in all com-missioning contracts that the commissions be produced at Henley, with this point being non-negotiable. These Henley facilities could be rebranded and repositioned, and the name could even be changed to something more purposeful and meaningful, as no one really knows what the significance and relevance of this name is.

• **Radio** – For some reason, radio appears to be one of the few resources with less drama and continues to sustain the public broadcaster. However, be that as it may, my only challenge with radio is how its airtime is priced.

In my view, the public broadcasting radio offering is by far the most underpriced offering on the market. It makes no sense that platforms with a national footprint and more than 7 million listeners still make less income than regional radio stations who don't even have 1 million listeners. Something is off. Either the advertising industry doesn't value the black African audience as a credible market with buying power they can advertise to, or the sales team within the public broadcasting enterprise is lazy and is doing the bare minimum to hunt for new business and elevate revenue margins. Or perhaps the conspiracy theorist in me can conclude that the problem emanates from the fact that most of the products and advertising brands the public broadcaster wants on its platforms are owned by the same people who own the competing media broadcast companies, and, therefore, they prefer to shift the slice of the advertising pie to their own broadcast platforms instead.

This assertion suggests that perhaps the public broadcaster ought to strategically think outside the idea of advertising being the 'magic wand' that can turn its revenue woes around, and instead begin to orchestrate its business model towards dealing directly with the customers as opposed to a dying business-to-business transactional model, a thought that leads me to my next area of orchestration, which is OTT.

• **OTT** – Over-the-top media offerings are a media streaming frenzy that has taken the broadcast landscape by storm for the last couple of years. This is yet another seismic shift that has resulted in rapid technological changes and media business discontinuities, leaving public broadcasting enterprises outdated, irrelevant, and uncompetitive, as the majority of content consumers are now spoilt for choice and forever seeking convenience, speed, and cost effectiveness, which OTT platforms can provide. Younger generations have walked away from traditional appointment-viewing business models, instead seeking high-quality and high production value content wherever, whenever, and on any device they choose.

The public broadcaster has indeed made its own foray into OTT content with the introduction of the SABC+ platform, which has actually improved drastically since its inception, attracting a significant number of consumers during the 2023 Rugby World Cup and 2024 Africa Cup of Nations (AFCON). However, the public broadcaster has still failed to use this platform to its full potential by effectively commercialising it, with more money being funneled into it than is being generated from it, and it boggles my mind why this platform even exists if it doesn't generate any income for the broadcaster. This was a noble idea gone wrong, in my opinion. An idea which I believe is a wasted opportunity and could have been a game changer. But, again, that is the price of employing unqualified non-professionals in strategic positions of influence.

Perhaps to salvage the spilled milk, it wouldn't hurt to continue with this SABC+ effort but improve its capabilities and just make it a direct replica of what is on the traditional linear offering, being explicit about the fact that it is not offering anything new, but is just a platform of convenience for those who want to watch the public broadcaster's programs on the go. Then, the broadcaster could implement a new, idiosyncratic OTT platform that will actually be of commercial value to the business, offering exclusive, high-quality content that people across

Africa can subscribe to at a pre-determined fee. The existing platform can even be used to promote it and sell it across the continent. Diversification strategies discussed earlier could also be implemented where the platform includes SVOD, TVOD, and AVOD, with an alternative continental Afrocentric news offering that could counter the Eurocentric agenda and propaganda advocated for by existing private media houses in the interest of the western capitalist conglomerates.

• **Education** – Currently, the public broadcaster has an "Education" department which falls in the content hub division and has dual responsibilities, namely in the marketing and outreach programs and in the content space as both a genre and an editorial oversight on some of the content that is classified as educational. However, all the other genres of the public broadcaster (such as drama, entertainment, children's content, religion, etc.) already carry with them their own mandate of delivering educational elements within their respective genres, so why is there a need to also have a separate education department within the content division? This is the most redundant department I've ever seen, and yet it continues to enjoy funding from the communications department for doing God knows what.

My proposition is to dismantle this façade of a department and instead treat education for exactly what it is— education. What most people don't know is that education in a developing country is a huge business, where some of the enterprises in the business of education are even listed on the Johannesburg Stock Exchange. I would rebrand the entire division and develop a new public media broadcasting school that focuses on reconciling the paradox between the public broadcasting service mandate and commercial broadcasting expectation. This could be a school that offers creative programs for public service media, editorial education, regulation and governance for public media managers, and executive leadership programs for public media enterprises, as well as broadcasts technology and engineering programs or short courses. These could be delivered on a blended mode, with masterclasses that can be purchased online, anywhere on the globe, to generate revenue.

2. Strategy Diversification – Apart from the OTT offering and education business the public broadcaster can explore, I am not sure, from a regulation perspective, what is stopping it from using its commercial license to diversify to financial services and capitalise off of its existing captive audience across TV and radio networks by selling life cover, funeral cover, and micro-loans to its loyal viewers. This can underwrite any of the existing financial institutions and generate additional revenue independent of the current (insufficient) advertising model.

The shareholders' idea to replace TV licenses with a tax is another game changer for the broadcaster that could also pivot them towards an unprecedented tier of revenue and afford them the sports rights that have been corruptly monopolised by private media enterprises in the interests of the few individuals on their payroll and those in collusion with government officials to maintain the status quo.

3. Corporate Rebranding – Contrary to the popular idea perpetuated by the mainstream private media that the public broadcasting enterprises are incompetent and useless, you will be surprised to learn that most of the public broadcaster's problems and what it is accused of have nothing to do with its core business of content. Most of the time, the organisation suffers reputational damage resulting from boardroom shenanigans and politically oriented problems.

Based on this assertion, I then argue that perhaps, together with all the aforementioned interventions for the new leadership, performing a full diagnostic exercise in the first six months and developing a completely new business strategy could be the most ambidextrous thing the broadcaster can do in order to keep the sheep afloat and overcome the current state of competitive disadvantage it once again finds itself in.

Now, this will come with unpopular decisions that will rack the cage and antagonise the beneficiaries of this corrupt public broadcasting system, and whoever takes up the mantle must brace themselves for resistance from all corners of the Earth, which includes employees, unions, board members, shareholders, suppliers, and the competition itself (not to mention the so-called NGOs who often pretend to be fighting for freedom of speech and the right to know, etc., and yet are on the payroll of capitalist interests that have no desire to see the public broadcasting enterprise compete and win).

One of the tough decisions to be made is the eradication of award shows on the public broadcasting television platforms, especially when they are still building their inventory and strengthening their content muscle. I never understood why the public broadcaster would license an award show that displays its competitors' programming winning on its own platform. It's the silliest thing I've ever seen, masqueraded as public interest. This is one of the ludicrous decisions I find bizarre; surely no one in their right mind and operating in the interests of the business would justify and agree to this. Witnessing your competitors' shows winning awards on your channel is essentially saying to your audience, "Stop watching my channel and go and watch my competitor, as they have the best shows on offer." This decision is tantamount to deliberate brand erosion, audience dilapidation, and revenue destruction. What is even sadder about these award shows is that they don't even generate sufficient audience ratings and have always delivered below the revenue projections, as they are infested with a plethora of commercial brands that paid the production company that is producing the show instead of the public broadcaster.

My proposition is that the public broadcaster creates its own award show. For example, it could invest in and strengthen the Metro FM awards and fight for its own advertising sponsorship, create its own traditional music awards led by Ukhozi FM, create its own gospel music awards led by Umhlobo Wenene FM, create its own hip-hop awards led by 5FM, and stop paying for under-performing licenses that add no value to its business and instead take away from it. Perhaps a 24/7 sports radio station could be created as an alternative to plugging the gap of not having a functional 24/7 sports channel on TV. A station such as Radio 2000 could be rebranded, repositioned, and reimagined in terms of what they are, who they're meant to serve, what their unique selling proposition is, and what the "2000" actually means or represents. The same could be said about Tru FM. If it is supposed to be a youth radio station for the public broadcaster, then it has to be intentional about it and stop operating as a community radio station. An application to get a license for a national footprint would not be a bad idea. The station could then rework its positioning and editorial direction with a composition of new on-air talent that broadcasts from different provinces and in different languages, while embracing the growing podcast culture and offering facilities and rental services across the country for young people wishing to create a show/

program at an affordable price. This would not only benefit the broadcaster financially by renting out spaces and producing this offering to the market, but it would also benefit it by tapping into the youth's headspace and having access to potential talent before anyone else while also gaining insights to what the youth thinks and wants—free empirical research in real time.

4. Dynamic Capabilities – For all these propositions to happen, the public broadcaster needs to master ordinary capabilities while also building new, dynamic capabilities. Furthermore, these dynamic capabilities should follow/align with perhaps the most accepted set of criteria for staying ahead of competition, which is Barney's VRIN (Valuable, Rare, Inimitable, and Non-substitutable), in order to be a source of sustainable competitive advantage.

A dynamic capability being 'valuable' implies that it creates something consumers have a willingness to pay for. Now, between you and me, we both know that the public broadcaster has struggled to make the public pay for TV licenses, which is the cheapest fee in the market compared to what other competing players are charging, which is a beyond-reasonable-doubt rejection and indication of how invaluable their product is.

'Rare', the second attribute of dynamic capabilities, acknowledges that the product of the capability has to be competitively superior. Now, once again, based on the public broadcaster's audience decline, market erosion, revenue depletion, and bankruptcy status, it is obvious that none of the public broadcaster's production offerings are deemed rare or exclusive by the consumer, not to mention the inferiority of the product quality they are selling at times.

The 'inimitability' test refers to the ease of direct replication of the dynamic capability by competitors. For the longest time, the public broadcaster has always cried and complained about copycat strategies being employed by the competition and the competition perfecting their blueprint. For example, the growth of local content acquisitions by private media broadcast networks, the newly introduced offering of *isiZulu* and *isiXhosa* news by private media broadcast networks, the growth of vernacular content on private media broadcast networks, and the full-on acquisition of sports rights that used to belong to the public broadcast enterprises—all these being just a few of the signs showing how easily imitable public broadcasting capabilities have been over the years.

Finally, the 'non-substitutability' test looks at the capability's vulnerability to replacement by a different capability or by a resource that satisfies the same demand by consumers at a lower cost or with a higher willingness to pay. The unfortunate substitutable nature of the public broadcaster's capabilities is evident in the fact that consumers are prepared and willing to pay what the competition is charging for their content rather than consume free content from the public broadcaster, an indication of how far down the barrel these enterprises have fallen.

According to literature, and as pioneered by David J. Teece, a professor at the Institute of Business Innovation at the University of California and the pioneer and founder of the Dynamic Capabilities theory, "dynamic capabilities as a concept are a firm's ability to build and integrate internal and external competencies during rapid changing environments," which means that in order for the public broadcaster to genuinely turn itself around, not only does it need to be corruption-free and embrace all the aforementioned generic and ordinary capabilities (which are the most basic of the broadcasting business, in my view), but it is required to also build new sensing, seizing, and configuring capabilities, thereby putting the creativity, innovation, and adaptability of public broadcasting enterprise operations at the center of the new turnaround strategy. This is, of course, notwithstanding the importance of adhering to the operational efficiencies, governance, regulatory remits, and editorial obligations that come with operating as a public service enterprise seeking self-sufficiency and commercial prosperity while delivering on its mandates to educate, inform, and entertain.

BOOK PUBLISHING ENTERPRISES

Contrary to the preceding section about linear and public broadcast enterprises where I strongly advocate for the strengthening and preservation of the public broadcasting enterprise concept in the interest of the public and the creative arts industry, the book publishing industry section is unfortunately where I pick up where I left off and once again say "cut out the 'middleman'". Book publishing enterprises are another evil yet sophisticated, under-the-radar 'boogeyman' accused of exploiting millions of authors across the globe—a different type of 'boogeyman' that is sometimes labelled as being even worse than the music industry.

Now, for an industry to be classified as being worse than the music industry, you must know the situation is beyond literary discussions. As in other arts sectors, the ultimate discussion inspiring the 'cut out the middleman' syndrome, even in the book publishing industry, is the imbalance of commercial transactions between the authors, publishers, and retail bookstores. This tug of war, at face value, is seen to be skewed towards the publishers. However, the real predators are in fact the bookstores, who leave the authors—who spent months sitting at their desks grinding the stories and spewing out the words onto paper—with only pennies and nickels. Once again, it is a debate inspired by technological discontinuities where readers no longer need to buy physical books like they used to in the past and can instead purchase books online and read them using a variety of electronic devices, including smartphones, tablets, and e-readers.

The standard practice in the book publishing industry is that royalties are often paid in gross sales as opposed to a minimum price per unit, meaning that the book publisher will refuse to set a minimum price per unit and rather insist on paying the author based on gross sales, essentially selling the book inventory or doing a wholesale to bookstores around the world with a price point determined by them per unit. This is a business model that often leave authors with almost nothing to justify all the hard work they have been putting in over the period of months, if not years, and it is an exploitative business deal that most authors argue is designed to screw writers over and give publishers free reign to do what they want with their intellectual property.

In this scenario, all the power and control is handed over to the publishers to do with as they please, creating a loophole in the author-publisher relationship that opens up a gap for some publishers to be dishonest about the price at which they sell units to different territories and rip off authors by striking separate private contracts with the book retailers at price points unknown to the authors. Although not all publishing houses are as scrupulous as the example outlined above, there is a growing number of authors who feel hard done by the publishers and are continuously looking for a way out of these blood-sucking deals.

However, like in any other industry, where there is chaos, there will always be opportunity. In book publishing, opportunity takes the form of the parallel industry of self-publishing which has now opened up and which has never existed before. An exciting seismic shift where authors no longer have to deal with the purported exploitative publishing 'boogeyman' that colludes and fixes prices with bookstores and subjects authors to poverty and indignity. The self-publishing phenomenon confirms assertions that the 'middleman' adds no value to the chain except to inflict pain to both writers and consumers for self-enrichment through inflated prices. As a result, even giant multinational conglomerates like Amazon have jumped on the bandwagon to plug the gap for those authors who don't want to deal with the book publishing 'boogeyman', offering services that enable authors to skip the 'middleman' and publish and market their books on Kindle, Nook, and iBooks (to name just a few) at a fraction of the price. This has simplified and demystified the notion that getting a book into print is a difficult process and that publishing a book from start to finish is a costly procedure, including expenses such as copy editing, printing, cover design, warehousing, delivery, and promotion.

The rapidly changing world of publishing and the revolution of e-book readers has made it possible for authors to skip the 'middleman' and still make a fortune from their work by easily and freely publishing their books themselves electronically. Whereas the thing that makes most authors publishing their books via the traditional route unsatisfied with the process is what they call 'book royalties'. Putting it simply, a book royalty is the amount of money that a book publisher pays an author for the rights to publish their book—a concept that appears straightforward and simple enough to follow, in my view—and the trade-off to this deal is the handing over of rights to publish the book to the publisher. The royalty split is calculated in a percentage format. For example, although the rates can vary from publisher to publisher, an author could potentially earn seven and a half percent royalties on every paperback sold and twenty -five percent on every e-book sold. Off the bat, you can tell that these numbers look suspicious and silly. If you ask me, this seems like a deal that is just as exploitative as music deals are towards musicians.

Like how musicians can make extra money through performances, endorsements, and other appearances, authors can also make additional money outside of book sales by giving talks, finding new clients, consulting, product launches, coaching, and podcasting. But these are extremely rare occasions and are often difficult to do for authors. Therefore, the game plan for authors is always simple: write books that you think are going to sell, and sell them to the largest audience possible.

If you are a first-time author like me, the royalty rates might look something like this (according to statistics from an article on book royalties by Scribe Media, a top U.S.-based publishing company):

- Hardcover sale: 15%
- Trade paperback sale: 7.5%
- Mass market paperback sale: 5%
- eBook Sale: 25%
- Audio Book Sale: 25%

Apparently, some contracts will also have deals known as graduated royalty deals. What that means is that you might earn ten percent on the first 5 000 copies of your book sold, twelve percent on the next 5 000 copies, and fifteen percent on every copy sold thereafter. Now, to simplify this book royalty concept even further, imagine your book is retailing at R400 and your royalty rate is five percent; this means that as an author, you will earn R20 per book sold. Sometimes, publishers may also pay authors according to model called "royalties on net sales." Essentially, publishers will sell to different book retailers at different prices (for example, they might offer a substantial discount to a retailer like Amazon that would be buying a large number of copies; whereas they would give less of a discount to a smaller, independent bookstore that would only buy a few copies), and royalties on net sales are calculated after factoring in all the price differences and discounts. Then there is another animal called an 'advance'. I am sure for musicians this will also sound familiar and painful, but for those who don't know what an advance is, it is a negotiable, upfront payment that a publisher would pay to the author before they actually publish the book.

If you are a big-shot author with a hot topic or are in demand with a large publisher, you might earn yourself a million-rand advance; however, most advances are not that generous. The logic behind the matrix is always based on projections of how well the publisher thinks the books will sell. Books that deal with highly relevant topics and are written by well-established authors will undoubtedly sell a lot of copies, which means the author would receive higher advance. On the flip side, books that deal with more specialised or unique topics and/or may be written by a lesser-known author will likely sell a much smaller number of copies, so the author would receive a much smaller advance.

In the same aforementioned article by Scribe Media about book royalties, advances are explained in more detail as follows:

> Advances aren't charitable gifts. They are payments against future royalties. That means if a publisher gives you a $100,000 advance, they expect to make more than $100,000 off book sales. Once an Author gets an advance, they won't see another cent until their book has sold enough copies to pay the advance back. In other words, if your book is earning royalties at a rate of $1 per copy, and you got a $100k advance, you'd have to sell more than 100,000 copies before you'd receive royalty payments. Advances are great if you can get them, but they're hard to get. Publishers want to know that a book is going to be a sure success before they give an Author an advance. […] Unless you already have thousands of followers on social media or a highly visible personal brand, it's hard to break into the world of traditional publishing. Publishers don't want to take risks, and most Authors don't have the platform to guarantee 25,000 sales.

The article also advises that even if you are lucky enough to score an advance, there are still several trade-offs to consider:

> You will no longer own the print license for your book, which means you can't do anything else with the content. If you wanted to break it into smaller chunks and sell it on your website, you couldn't. If you wanted to turn it into a magazine article, you'd have to get the publisher's permission. Then, if the book is a major hit, you're only going to get a small fraction of the profits. Let's say you earn back that $100k advance and sell

another 200,000 copies. With royalties, you'd earn another $100k. But if you had self-published that same book, you'd earn 100% on each sale after recouping your production costs. That's a lot more than 5%. Instead of $200,000, you could be making millions.

When you self-publish your book instead of traditionally publishing it, you keep the rights to your intellectual property. If we then apply this logic to self-publishing on Amazon, which I mentioned earlier, it means that, technically, Amazon's payments aren't really 'royalties' in the traditionally accepted sense of the word (even though Kindle Direct Publishing [KDP] still calls them that). For KDP books, authors can choose between two royalty options: thirty-five percent or seventy percent. While going for the higher percentage may seem like the obvious choice, there are some stipulations involved which may incline an author to consider the lower percentage, such as pricing and geographical availability. However, regardless of which royalty plan an author chooses, by publishing through the KDP system, they keep complete control over how much they want to charge for their books as well as how they want to promote them. Essentially, the authors have the right to use their books however they want to.

Now, being the first-time author that I am, and writing a book that advocates for cutting out the 'middleman', you can imagine the dilemma I find myself in. If one of the big global publishers had to come to me saying, "Here is a million-dollar advance," would I jump at the chance and sell out my idea of cutting out the 'middleman'? Or would I have to make a concession depending on how favourable the deal is? I guess I will cross that bridge when I get to it.

Despite all this, the idea of taking control of your intellectual property—even with all the financial risks and hard labour that come with doing it yourself—is an exciting prospect and an experience I don't want to miss out on regardless of the financial impact of the journey. In my view, the major difference between self-publishing and the traditional route is the fact that in traditional publishing, the publisher absorbs all the risks on behalf of the author in addition to all the logistical and administrative requirements of publishing and marketing the book, fostering relationships with book outlets and ensuring the professionalisation of the final product, all of these being activities that justify the percentage splits of the royalties. On the other hand, in self-publishing, you do everything on your own, meaning that this route may only work for you if you have a firm belief in yourself and your work, and if you already have all the necessary skills, resources, and capabilities traditional publishers have.

However, one thing I don't like about the traditional publishing route, and something which took me by surprise, is the fact that in some countries, they have institutionalised gatekeepers known as literary agents. I had never even heard of such a concept until I started writing this book. I think of this phenomenon as the systematic practice of striking down the hopes and dreams of ambitious writers who reach out directly to publishers with a hope of getting their books published, only to be informed that they need to go through a literary agent in order to be considered. This is a very 'boogeyman'-like behaviour that is similar to what Netflix does, where they don't accept any unsolicited proposals from film and television production houses they don't know or have never worked with before—essentially a "Don't call us, we'll call you" type of set up. Netflix prefers to work with a select few production companies that they know well and trust, and if you have a concept or pitch deck that you think is suitable for their platform, it's better to go through one of these companies or go through one of the agents they already deal with in order to stand a chance of being invited to a pitch. It is a phenomenon that is on the borderline of closed pitching and preferential procurement, and it has become a trend that private free media broadcasters and some popular private pay television networks have adopted recently, as I've addressed in previous chapters.

But anyway, back to the literary agents. Essentially, literary agents are the publisher's way of weeding out low-quality manuscripts (or so they say), invariably acting as the 'middleman' that vets authors or books before anything even gets near the publishers themselves. Basically, this process allows an agent's subjective opinion to determine whether the book will land on the publisher's desk or not. However, as suspect as this is, this is not even the real 'middleman' I want to focus on. In my view, publishing houses are the real 'middlemen' that I believe occupy the very same space major record labels, broadcast networks, and governments occupy in exploiting the creatives. A real 'middleman' that needs to be cut out, and I firmly believe that institutions such as Amazon and other big tech companies are strategically entering the market to plug in this gap.

The importance of finding new ways to distribute and market creative material online couldn't be stressed enough. If only a purported fifteen percent of book publishing costs goes to shipping and printing (if that even is the case), then where does the rest of the money go? With the advent of technology allowing everything to be uploaded online, publishers can no longer be the gatekeepers, except to play a role in focusing on how to add quality, something I am not even sure they can do since the definition of 'quality' is no longer what it used to be in the traditional sense of publishing, and even that has found new meaning.

Traditionally, what publishers classify as 'quality' is proofing of grammar, syntax, and consistency of usage—essentially obsessing over getting every comma and semi-colon right, ensuring that capitalisation is consistent, and so on and so forth. This is a key performance measure of what they would classify as making documents look professional and presentable, enforcing standards, and quantifying this effort as a valuable contribution to the quality of the book. Reading a sentence multiple times that's missing a word and having to go over it again and again just to see how the parts fit together, proofreading in order to see if there are any comprehension problems to be resolved, and double checking all the facts asserted by the author in the book while editing all unclear and ambiguous passages are just some of the steps taken in this quality control process.

Now, as important as the aforementioned contributions by the traditional publishers to the quality of the book may seem, the fundamental question for me is how much of today's reading market actually values that contribution in the era of forty-character messages on social media platforms like X (formerly Twitter). Does the effort of polishing grammar, spelling, and sentence construction justify the percentage split publishers take of the books' sales?

A publishing executive I once spoke to said to me that, actually, the real 'middlemen' that need to be cut out are not the book publishers but rather the bookstores, who are muscling publishers for exorbitant amounts of money with unrealistic percentage splits before the books are even sold. They employ a bullying business model that results in a domino effect where publishers are themselves forced to preserve their own bottom line in order to keep the business sustainable; otherwise, what would be the point of even being in the business?

This ripple effect passes itself down to the authors and unfortunately creates the impression that they are being exploited by the publishers; whereas the real abusers and exploiters are the book retailers, which is a scenario that is no different from the picture I painted in earlier chapters about creatives and film and television production houses that are all abused and bullied by the broadcasters. There are even allegations of bookstore owners who collude with some publishers to push the books coming from publishers they don't have relationships with to the back of the shelf, reserving the front shelves for their preferred publishing houses—a very sneaky operation that is highly concentrated and manipulated by the select few who possess the right connections with the right retailers.

This is a very corrupt system that is similar to all forms of the creative arts and media industries. Apart from the readers and writers, publishing is indeed made up of 'middlemen', with retail mediators on one side and arbiters of taste and merit on the other. With the idea of publishers not only honing and polishing your manuscript relentlessly on your behalf but also marketing and publicising your book after the fact, you would think that there is nothing fundamentally wrong with the model until you realise how rigged and broken everything actually is. Authors such as Guy Kawasaki and Tim Ferriss have proved that the new dawn of the publishing era has arrived, and perhaps the tipping point that marks the demise of traditional publishing as we know it has landed upon us. This is a prime time to cut this traditional publishing 'middleman' out while at the same time being wary of the new 'middleman' in the form of multinational tech conglomerates. As sexy as this might sound, though, the elephant in the room will always be ownership of the production and distribution means of the product, as is the case for musicians and film and television producers.

More often than not, musicians can't afford to book time in a studio to record their songs, but airtime on radio and television stations is how musicians need to market and brand themselves to larger audiences who will access and purchase the music, and this requires professional recordings. Similarly, many producers can't afford to book film studios, rent production equipment, and hire cast and crew to produce their creative concept and tell their story so that they can license professional productions to broadcast networks for viewers to access their content. The same is true for authors too. Authors themselves can't afford to hire professionals to take care of the literary work of professionalising the book, fact checking and researching the work, designing the look and feel of the book, and printing the units of the book, let alone negotiating with the distribution outlets in the form of bookstores for the sales, marketing, and promotion of the book.

This is a phenomenon that leaves authors with no choice but to approach publishers who have all the resources to handle the aforementioned challenges, which is an advisable option for a first-time writer who still wishes to make a name for themselves as a credible author. Contrary to popular belief that book sales are declining and the South African market is not really a reading one, I'm probably one of the few optimists who believes that his book in particular will sell in insane numbers. Perhaps the problem faced by many authors struggling to sell copies of their book lies in the strength of the book concept they are launching to the market, the sensitivity and controversy that comes with the topics addressed by the book, and most importantly, the marketing strategy they employ in ensuring that the book flies off the shelves. As a broadcaster, and with my creative marketing experience, I strongly believe that *The Middleman with Power* will break new boundaries and demystify the notion of South Africans being a nation that doesn't read, and I have a goal to sell a million copies in the first year of release. I will never forget my friend's laughter when I mentioned this figure. He was almost short of calling me delusional, arguing that the best-selling books in this country doesn't even exceed 20 000 copies, yet I'm coming here, as a first-time author, talking about 1 million copies. "Get out of here!" he'd said, and I remember my last words just being, "Watch me."

However, all jokes aside, and despite my assertions about cutting out the 'middleman' and creatives embracing digital technologies to sell directly to their customers, the book publishing part of me believes that for a first-time author like myself, perhaps it is prudent to use a publishing house in order to benefit from the experienced team of professionals that come with it, and for a branding purposes, I also believe that it is good for your brand and can help you avoid overhead costs as an author.

But this still does not discount the fact that for decades and decades, speculations have been making the rounds in literary arts corridors about major traditional publishing houses being tight-lipped about book sales, royalties, how many books they actually sell, and why some book deals are into the millions of rands while others only sell but a mere handful, if any at all. Like the music industry, where artists are encouraged to do this for the sheer love of art and anything other than that seems to relegate you as something less of a true artist and being in it for the wrong reasons, the publishing industry is no different. On the same token, mainstream media wants to make people believe that there is no money in the publishing industry, and less still in South Africa where the culture of reading is nothing to write home about. The conspiracy theorist in me would like to argue that perhaps this is a scam peddled to discourage people from pursuing this industry or to keep it elitist and concentrated in orientation while brainwashing authors into believing that writing a book is for a good cause and not for profit maximisation. However, despite all the above outlined conspiracy theories about the book publishing industry, don't lose your groove. Continue to cultivate your own voice and craft a way to tell your stories in a way that millions will want to read badly enough to pay for.

5

THE IMBALANCE

With the advent of technology and new distribution channels to push creative artists' and media professionals' work to larger audiences, creative artists of all disciplines need to learn to master the instruments of business in order to make money. Creative industries are the types of industries that love power, and the balance of that power has drastically shifted quite expeditiously, completely disrupting the market with the influx and rapid proliferation of digital technology. It has become a tug of war among the 'middleman' enterprises which is nowhere ending, so long as creative artists remain on the sidelines and in the periphery of financial decisions involving their craft, while the 'boogeyman' takes centre stage and pulls all the stops to fight for the control, ownership, and distribution rights of the artists' creative work (which it played no part in producing) and sell it to the highest bidder and the largest audience possible.

As is the case in the music industry with the introduction of new streaming platforms, and the book publishing industry with self-publishing online platforms, television broadcasting markets have also been going through their own period of industrial reform. Digital technologies have broken down traditional boundaries between information technology (IT), telecom, and media worlds, and have lowered barriers for new players to enter the production and distribution business of television programming. Like other media industries, television broadcasting has been highly affected by the digitisation wave that enables a convergence of players to explore new business opportunities and address disruptive challenges across the value chain. The far-reaching integration of broadcast content with broadband delivery platforms—exemplified by the rise of over-the-top (OTT) television platforms (i.e., Netflix, Hulu, and BBC iPlayer) and Connected TV devices—has allowed opportunities to bypass established distributors and destabilise mainstream business models.

The television industry is facing turbulent economic times marked by an increased level of market competition and a lower degree of profitability—a set of interrelated structural market evolutions that has been eroding the advertising-based business model most television broadcasters used to depend on. Not only have television advertising markets fallen dramatically during the tough economic times, but audience fragmentation has also added its own challenge to increased channel competition. Additionally, time-shifted viewing and ad-skipping phenomena have further affected the foundations of ad-supported business models.

These market shifts have resulted in tainted power relations within the creative arts industry and the media ecosystems, thereby creating an environment where structural processes of control over production, distribution, and consumption have transformed into battleground warfare between the producers and the distributors, with a tipping scale favouring the distributors more and artists being the collateral damage. In the book publishing industry, this battle would be between the publishers and the book outlets while authors are suffering. In the music industry, it would be between the major record labels and the streaming platforms while musicians are suffering. In the broadcast industry, it would be between the film and television production houses and the broadcast networks while the talent and crew suffer. This is a phenomenon I view as an indicator of the concentration of power in the creative arts industry across the globe, with perpetual structural inequalities of capitalist market systems pretending to be socialist creative business environments.

These are monopolistic power dynamics of greed and exploitation with no desire to serve authentic storytelling and promotion of self-expression to customers, and rather a desire to exert market power and control over the industry's scarce and essential resources. However, the validity of the scarcity debate is a discussion for another day, with some believing it's a fallacy and a man-made construct to separate the rich from the poor or to make the rich richer and the poor poorer, as well as being a mechanism to control the economic performance of the industries by aligning their dependence on the scarcity or availability of resources.

Ownership and control of these scarce resources allows enterprises to play a gatekeeper role in the market, a scenario that is so familiar in both the broadcast media and creative arts industries. Therefore, cutting out the 'middleman' and rapidly adopting new digital media technologies will then tip the economic scale of the creative arts industries towards artists and creative practitioners, who are the original producers of the content everyone is fighting over. The conferred power of the media and creative arts industries is essentially over the distribution channels, which are the only things that can make or break the 'middleman' autonomy. This is exactly where the alternative economic rents reside and are protected through copyrights and intellectual property laws.

This book does not only awaken the power of creative artists in the form of actors, musicians, authors, and the public at large. This book also seeks to awaken the giant inside small creative arts and media enterprises—such as film and television production houses, independent record labels, and independent publishing houses—that supply goods and services to the 'middlemen' (i.e., bookstore retailers, broadcast networks, governments, and big record labels known as the 'majors') and get them to push back and use technology to carve their own paths and develop their own distribution channels in order to swing the imbalanced scale of power back to where it belongs—with the artists. It is no secret that distributors have gained enormous economic power over the years at the expense of creatives, authors, and content producers. Nicholas Garnham, the head of the Media Studies School of Communication and Director of the Centre of Communication and Information at Westminster University, once argued that, "It is cultural distribution, not cultural production, that is the key locus of power and profit." An assertion that every creative artist of every discipline across the globe should take to heart and live by.

Garnham further lamented that, because the business of cultural goods is as much about "creating audiences" as it is about "producing cultural artifacts", distribution is characterised by the highest level of capital intensity, ownership concentration, and multi-nationalisation. Distributors act as gatekeepers, controlling access and bundling programming to commoditised audiences—a factual *modus operandi* of the media broadcasting and creative arts industry in any country in the world—and the only way of surviving it is by either killing them, joining them, or dying as paupers, as we have seen happening unabated across the globe.

Furthermore, economic power in the creative arts industry, and specifically in the broadcast media industry, resides with only a few private and public enterprises that have oligopolistic control over the delivery of cultural productions. This can be referred to as an 'hourglass' structure of media industries (many producers, few distributors) that is prevalent in the African continent. It is a concentration of ownership that results in power asymmetry, with relations of power skewed towards distributors and broadcasters highly depending on delivery networks controlled by multichannel operators, which leaves the film and television production house enterprises begging for business and willing to do anything and everything to get commissions and licensing deals regardless of how toxic and parasitic they are.

Hence, corruption, bribery, and collusion are the order of the day and evident in the quality of productions you see on screen from the same production houses, or in the quality of the same songs on high rotation on national radio stations coming from the same record labels (if the music industry analogy is anything to go by). Furthermore, the imbalances that manifest in the creative arts industry are a cancer that everyone is pretending doesn't exist, and if anyone does acknowledge it, they are accused of being a disgruntled practitioner who can't 'wing' their way to the circle. This invisible evil gives birth to ills such as social inequality, labour market failures, and outright discrimination that results in many creative jobs remaining exclusive and prevents talented, working-class people from making it.

It is not a secret that in South Africa, low pay and work insecurity, the cost of education, and proximity to political networks and nepotism all influence who gets a chance and who doesn't, especially when it comes to the state-owned and controlled enterprises and agencies. Not to mention cadre deployment, which is another insane idea that has destroyed all spheres of government while wiping out every state-owned enterprise the apartheid government ever built pre-1994. This man-made economic imbalance culminates as a result of incompetent, underqualified politicians that seem to destroy everything they lay their hands on, eroding the sustainability of the arts ecosystem and driving a lot of artists to run their own spaces and smaller, non-commercial, not-for-profit ventures which are practically impossible to turn into competitive enterprises that can compete globally and export their craft to foreign markets. In the absence of ethical and corruption-free leadership in South Africa, this book's position to cut out these 'boogeymen' from all areas of economic activity is vindicated.

6

#So whART?

The general notion of artists being poor, and their socioeconomic situation of uncertainty, has been debated for decades—a precarious state of affairs wherein they are smiling and raking in the big bucks one month and are broke and struggling to put food on the table the next month. Given this economic status, most economists will argue that artists choose poverty, and the biggest rationale that underpins this behaviour is that artists are born creative professionals, imagining and envisaging a dream of being compensated for their low incomes through non -monetary forms of remuneration such as enjoyment, fulfilment, and status. An implicit opinion that flows through from a trade exchange where artists are willing to exchange money for other rewards or benefits.

As unpopular as this might sound, artists are generally not the type of people that estimate and weigh their life-long financial income and non-monetary income against considering overall costs of, among other things, train-ing—a notion that confirms the fact that the hardship of artists is real and considerable. Whereas, according to Professor Hans Abbing:

> In the case of excited young artists, the low in-come may be somewhat compensated, but only a few years after leaving Art school, compensation

starts to diminish. Whereas an average lawyer is neither poor nor unsuccessful, most artists are poor, regard themselves as unsuccessful, and are regarded by others as unsuccessful as well. This does not worry starting artists but over time, many artists start to consider themselves failures, although they will not admit this openly.

Despite the challenges outlined in previous chapters about the creative arts and broadcast industries, compounded with a litany of well-orchestrated shackles that continue to impoverish artists and creative work professionals across all disciplines in the hands of the 'middlemen', it is also an undeniable fact that the creative arts industry is one that is growing four times faster than any other sector in the world, a phenomenon which suggests that training in the creative arts industry is also fast becoming a gateway for some of the most exciting, glamorous, and well-paid career paths. However, this is only the case if there are no corrupt and parasitic 'middleman' enterprises that are abusing and capitalising on the naivety and ignorance of many creative artists and playing on the artists' dedication to soldier on despite the previously mentioned precarities and their willingness to be poor and possibly fail—sacrificing themselves, time, and money and rejecting commerce in the name of art.

Be that as it may, regardless of what industry one is ploughing their trade in, one sure thing is that every organisation needs creative and conceptual individuals to interpret and operationalise its strategies to drive business imperatives forward. Creativity is a prerequisite in the advertising and marketing industries and one of the most desirable skills employers look for. It is also a valuable commodity to set candidates apart and a strategic bargaining tool to negotiate fair salaries with employers.

However, the artists' low-income earnings and amount of commitment and dedication given to art not only far exceed the overall private and public support given to them, but they also create a gap for the 'middleman' to abuse and exploit their generosity and associate the high value of art with the image of poverty, which almost paints a picture that the symbolic value of art would be lower and the association with art would bring less distinction if the artists actually earn well. These are sad narratives which suggest that, based on the orientation of the industry and how it has always been positioned, poverty is perhaps something that should remain among artists as a symbolic value of distinction, while artists look and are perceived as rich, famous superstars swimming in the splendour of glitz and glamour. I mean, we have stood witness to artists bragging about how they've earned their stripes to be where they are in the game and often referring to how they used to busk in the streets for survival or do street theatre, unintentionally painting these scenarios as 'cool' and what moulded their craft; hence, they are where they are today.

Another reason artists are accused of being complicit in the exploitation and abuse that they experience from the industry 'middleman' is that they reproduce the economic exploitation they face single-handedly by helping those who see this as a commercial gap to plug. The fact that commerce is denounced, denied, covered up, and at times condemned by artists in the art business is a self-inflicted problem that artists are oblivious about, and they should take responsibility for the commercial deprivation they could have enjoyed should any of the aforementioned practices not be veiled and masqueraded as vocation and passion. But fortunately, the creative arts industry remains one of the lucrative industries that is growing exponentially, more so now with the develop-

156

ment of digital technology and everyone taking matters into their own hands by cutting out the 'middleman' and producing and distributing their own content straight to the consumer.

The 2021 Deloitte annual report states that, "The creative economy is an ecosystem that comprises a wide range of occupations distinguished by the generation of wealth and jobs through individual creativity driving the generation and use of intellectual property." This includes the creative industries such as film and TV, publishing, museums, music and performing arts, computer programming, crafts, architecture, and design.

This staggering report raises the question of why artists continue to be poor if the industry is growing and generating wealth and jobs through *their* creativity and intellectual property. The report highlighted that the creative economy is indeed large and growing. In the study conducted in nine economies in Europe (UK, Germany, France, Türkiye, Italy, and Spain), approximately 20 million people were employed. Deloitte argues that this is indicative of what is likely to be a key driver of economic growth over the long term, especially when governments worldwide look to rebuild their economies in the wake of the downturn associated with COVID-19.

The creative arts economy is a new-knowledge economy capable of revitalising depressed areas of the general economy and building cultural heritage. While many other sectors are suffering, creative individuals blend culture and technology to generate jobs and build organisations based on social value and inclusion. This industry has abundant renewable resources, using knowledge, experience, and imagination to generate value and create goods and services that can often be developed, bought, sold, and delivered online. It doesn't take a rocket scientist to figure out that those who own the production and distribution means of content, and those who hold the gatekeeping power to determine who enters and exits the industry, don't want artists to speak out about these shenanigans that are at play in the creative arts industry. Understandably so, as such conversations do not benefit the existing establishments and are detrimental to the sustainability and perpetual maintenance of the status quo.

Hence, it is in every capitalist's interest to ensure that such discussions and allegations of abuse and artist exploitation are rubbished and removed immediately while also painting artists who are bold enough to speak out about them as being problematic and difficult to work with. If there was ever a need for artists to rise up, that need or time is now, including those operating both in front of and behind the camera. The creative arts fraternity needs to grow in numbers and in defence of what they believe they are called for. It's time for them to start operating differently, strive for various goals that propel them to greater heights, and transform themselves from the vocation syndrome into the entrepreneurial and market-oriented way of doing business. That begins by ensuring that everything they do is aimed at owning and controlling the distribution channels and cutting out the 'middleman' by transacting directly with their customers. However, to achieve this transformation, everything needs to start with the education system that prepares these creatives and supplies the market with the voca-tional output of professionals brainwashed to believe that this is a calling and is for 'the love of art', as this mindset results in everyone except for the artists themselves bene-fitting from the art and enjoying the splendour of the proceeds that emanates from the artists' sweat and blood.

In 2017, Dr Marco Thom, who is a renowned scholar of the arts business, once said that art entrepreneurship, art market structure, and the relationship between artists and buyers/intermediaries are critical areas of research that need special attention across the globe. He emphasises the importance of understanding the term 'entrepreneurship' as it relates to the arts, and further asserts that being a practising artist (whether you are commercially motivated or not) should have nothing to do with "oppression and modern slavery" and should not be dependent on governmental subsidies to survive professionally. This circumstance is socially and economically worrying and calls for urgent change. Nevertheless, individual artists are still a necessity, if not the most important component, in a thriving arts ecosystem. Creating a social environment in which practising artists can make a living without subsidies and multiple job holdings, and thrive artistically with an appropriate social reputation, is necessary to ensure a sustainable, healthy art economy.

Research shows that the rapid growth of the creative arts and media economies is an unstoppable machine, as the consumption of artistic material never stops. The only changes become the platforms and distribution channels through which the content is consumed, which are based on technological superiority in terms of convenience, speed, affordability, and quality of content. This should be more than convincing to creative artists and media practitioners that their value and the need for artistic goods and services will always be there; they just need to expand the market and be as independent as they can be, take their power back, and cut out the 'middleman' by any means necessary in order to shape their own destiny and express their artistic prowess freely and independently without censorship or exploitation.

ABOUT THE AUTHOR

Phumzile Zonke is an Executive Creative Producer, public broadcast strategist, public media consultant, and a former SABC Head of Channel (TV). He is also a multi-award-winning Gold PromaxBDA Africa recipient and is celebrated as one of the country's leading creatives and public broadcast intellectuals, with twenty-five years of professional experience in the media entertainment industry (radio, television, and theatre). He currently runs a startup media production and distribution company that provides audio-visual solutions to clients, strategy consultancy for public media enterprises, and creative business workshops to creative artists and students.

He is a creative entrepreneur, writer, and researcher who is studying towards a PhD degree with research focused on the evolutionary fitness of public broadcast enterprises across the globe. Mr Zonke holds an Executive Leadership qualification from Saïd Business School at the University of Oxford, Master of Philosophy in International Business from Gordon Institute of Business Science (GIBS) at the University of Pretoria, Master of Business Administration (MBA) from Monash University, and Bachelor of Arts in Media, Communications, and Culture from Nelson Mandela University.

The Middleman With Power is a book inspired by Mr Zonke's experiences as a creative artist and executive manager that ploughed his trade in radio, film and television, theatre, and now literary work.